Additional Praise for
Pathway to Purpose:
Big Ideas for Fueling Irresistible Corporate Cultures

"It's one thing to wax poetic about being a workplace of excellence. It's another thing altogether to demonstrate how it can actually be accomplished in a real-world, corporate setting. Jamey Lutz has a proven track record of helping organizations design irresistible cultures that employees and customers alike find simply irresistible. If you are serious about taking your culture to the next level, make *Pathway to Purpose* required reading for all your leaders!" – **Lisa McLeod, bestselling author,** *Selling with Noble Purpose*

"Jamey is a workplace culture anthropologist, drawing on his extensive experience in organizational development, culture, and leadership. Jamey has a passion for learning and an even greater passion for helping others find joy and fulfillment in their work. *Pathway to Purpose* is an inspirational account of Jamey's journey, collected through a successful career and relevant life experiences. Whether speaking one-on-one or to an audience of five hundred, Jamey connects the dots from these experiences for the reader in an inspiring and actionable way." – **Annette Rollins, EVP, Chief Human Resources Officer, Atlantic Capital Bank**

"I think the most important prefix in the English language is **RE.** To re-commit, re-envision, and re-imagine is the best way to be creative and transformative in today's fast paced world. My friend, Jamey Lutz, challenges his readers to re-think the way they look at work by looking at how others create excellence and add value to their work. When you link your personal skill set to a noble purpose then passion is the result...when passion reigns then the ordinary becomes extraordinary! Buy this book, implement the timeless values and you can help change your world!" – **Dr. Dwight "Ike" Reighard, President/CEO MUST Ministries**

"*Pathway to Purpose* is a comprehensive guide for those interested in leveraging the power of human capital—a must-read for leaders looking to unlock the secrets of employee engagement and achieve high profitability levels. Jamey does a splendid job of sharing best practices and practical tips that can be easily implemented by companies of all sizes. His engaging style of writing made this an easy and enjoyable read." – **Roberta Matuson, President, Matuson Consulting and author of *Can We Talk?***

"When you think of companies with incredible cultures, that are also among the absolute best places to work, you think of the Ritz Carlton, the NBA's Orlando Magic, and Atlantic Capital Bank. It is no surprise that Jamey Lutz had leadership roles with each, playing pivotal roles in developing cultures of excellence and incredible work environments. *Pathway to Purpose* provides us with the historical perspective, his experiences and knowledge, and a peek into Jamey's playbook to help all of us apply what we can learn and use in our own companies and workplace." – **Roy Heintz, National Director of Service Excellence, Reliable Roofing**

"We live in a world of exceptional or nothing. As such, creating a culture of purpose and excellence becomes the new competitive advantage. Jamey Lutz has crafted a well-researched case for living by purpose in work and life, and he has charted the operational blueprint to transform your culture and activate the intrinsic motivation of your people. The first step in winning the hearts and minds of your people, is reading this important book." – **Lior Arussy, author of *Customer Experience Strategy, Exceptionalize It!* and *Next is Now!***

"Why is it that so many organizations aspire to become employers of choice but never quite get there? As Jamey Lutz points out in his new book, great cultures don't just happen by chance. They arise when leaders make a concerted commitment to prioritizing people over profit. *Pathway to Purpose* delivers on a set of guiding principles that will inspire your employees to perform at their collective best." – **Sonny Deriso, Chairman, Atlantic Capital Bank**

"*Pathway to Purpose* serves as a roadmap of practical strategies to turn your workplace into a cultural powerhouse. Jamey Lutz's plan for designing world-class cultures is backed by a proven mix of validated research and personal experience. This is a book you will want to read, re-read and gift to a friend." **– Chester Elton, Executive Coach, author of *Leading with Gratitude* and *The Carrot Principle***

"In *Pathway to Purpose*, Jamey Lutz connects the dots for how to create or transform an organization in a way that empowers it to prosper with the right combination of strong core values, an inspiring team culture, high performance standards, and strategies for fulfilling its mission. Through an effective combination of research and personal experience, Jamey provides concepts, principles, actionable steps and specific examples for making 'irresistible culture' a reality." **– Richard Tiller, Executive Coach, co-author of *Motivation from the Heart***

PATHWAY TO PURPOSE

PATHWAY
TO **PURPOSE**

*Big Ideas for Fueling **Irresistible** Corporate **Cultures***

You only live once. Live on
Purpose !

JAMEY B. LUTZ

Charleston, SC
www.PalmettoPublishing.com

Pathway to Purpose
Big Ideas for Fueling Irresistible Corporate Cultures
Copyright © 2021 by Jamey Lutz

All rights reserved

First Edition

Hardcover ISBN: 978-1-64990-136-1
Paperback ISBN: 978-1-64990-923-7
eBook ISBN: 978-1-64990-598-7

TABLE OF CONTENTS

INTRODUCTION

Irresistible

Looking back more than two decades ago, I distinctly remember making the three-hour drive from Orlando to South Florida to interview for a senior leadership position at the Ritz-Carlton, Palm Beach. To say I was excited would be an understatement. Even at this early stage of my career, I was fascinated by how certain companies manage to create an almost cultlike following in the marketplace...the type of company that fanatical customers flock to in droves and gladly dispense of their hard-earned cash, the type of company that employees incessantly brag about to their friends and family, and the type of company that is the topic of countless lectures and dissertations from the top business schools in the country. Indeed, I wanted to understand why such a tiny fraction of enterprises reach the pinnacle of performance excellence, while most businesses remain mired in mediocrity.

Few companies have demonstrated long-term excellence and staying power like the Ritz-Carlton Hotel Company, an organization that, at this point in its history, has already earned a global reputation for being both an exceptional place to work and an unquestioned leader in the art of customer service. At the time of my Ritz interview, I was working in a middle-management role for RDV Sports, the parent company of the Orlando Magic NBA basketball team.

I had a very cool job, with a significant portion of my responsibilities centered on developing strategies to enhance the external season-ticket holder / fan experience while internally driving higher levels of employee engagement. Our organization had become familiar with Ritz's consistently outstanding service levels, regularly lodging at available properties as part of ongoing team and business travel. Over time, we had the good fortune to meet with numerous members of the Ritz senior leadership team to learn how to better translate their best practices to the sports and entertainment industry.

With the pristine backdrop of the Atlantic Ocean coastline and a bird's-eye view of the immaculately maintained resort grounds, I anxiously sat in the grand lobby that beautiful summer day for my much-anticipated interview with general manager Wolfgang Baere, a renowned hotelier and one of the founding fathers of Ritz-Carlton. I was a nervous wreck!

The embodiment of old-school German swagger and sophistication, Mr. Baere had a commanding presence about him that was simultaneously inspiring *and* terrifying. His voice boomed when he spoke, and he made two things extremely clear from the outset of our discussion. Number one, he reminded me that achieving anything great in business (and life) requires great commitment and sacrifice. Mr. Baere viewed his role, and that of every Ritz employee, as a noble calling, not just a job. "We are ladies and gentlemen serving ladies and gentlemen," he said with resolute conviction. "What we do matters, and we have a collective responsibility to uphold the great legacy of Ritz-Carlton. When you step foot on property as a Ritz-Carlton team member, you represent the very finest in hospitality. Mediocrity is not acceptable here." He went on to say that working at Ritz-Carlton was not for everyone, that it demanded bringing your best self to the job every single day, even when your mind and body might try to convince you otherwise.

Secondly, Mr. Baere emphasized that a passion for service was a prerequisite for success at Ritz-Carlton. "It's not about you, and it's not about me," he said. "At the end of the day, everything rests on us taking exceptional care of our guests. As long as our actions never cross the line into the realm of unethical, illegal, or immoral, we will move heaven and earth to surprise and delight them. If you don't genuinely care about serving the spoken and unspoken needs of our customers and teammates, you will not survive here."

As the interview with Mr. Baere wound down, and I proceeded to meet with additional executive team members that day, it became increasingly clear that the mystique I had heard so much about over the years through case studies, books, and university lectures was not just hyperbole or some grandiose folklore. There was an authentic vibe within the hotel and larger organization that I was unable to put my finger on at the time. But as I would discover over the coming weeks and years (yes, I got the job!), the Ritz culture is uniquely special. It is not perfect, of course, but it is refreshingly different, even to the point of being...*irresistible.*

Throughout the course of my career, I have become increasingly convinced that it is absolutely possible to design workplace cultures that authentically reflect the collective mission and purpose of the company's employees. In the pages ahead, I will lay the groundwork for developing a pathway to purpose in your organization. Together, we will explore a set of cultural mandates that when properly embraced set the stage for an irresistible and unstoppable workplace.

Sound idealistic? It's not. There are numerous current-day examples (beyond Ritz-Carlton) of irresistible cultures already thriving in the marketplace. As you will see, they come in relatively all shapes and sizes: large and small; new businesses and long-established ones; public and private; for-profit and not-for-profit. Take Nordstrom, the legendary upscale department store founded in 1901 that has grown to more than seventy-four thousand employees. Over the course of its history, Nordstrom has successfully navigated (and embraced) the growing trend toward e-commerce while also avoiding the unnecessary corporate bureaucracy that has crippled so many current and former competitors. At Nordstrom, the employee handbook amazingly covers just one rule: "Use your best judgment in all situations. There will be no additional rules."[1]

Or consider relative newcomer King of Pops, an Atlanta-based company that makes all-natural, great-tasting ice pops (think popsicles but better) in literally hundreds of amazing flavors, including banana puddin', blackberry ginger lemonade, and chocolate sea salt. In 2010, brothers Steven and Nick Carse officially launched their new enterprise, peddling pops from a used ice-cream cart in the parking lot of a local gas station. Word spread quickly, and by 2015, King of Pops had begun selling its refreshing treats at Atlanta Braves home baseball games. Fast-forward, and the company has since expanded retail operations to various locations in Georgia, Tennessee, the Carolinas, and Virginia.

As an interesting extension of King of Pops, the Carse brothers developed a sixty-eight-acre farm (a.k.a. King of Crops) in Douglasville, Georgia, to source many of their own ingredients, build closer community ties, and educate others about sustainable farming practices. Based upon the growing clamor among customers and employees alike surrounding this uniquely positioned enterprise, King of Pops is well on its way to becoming a cultural exemplar.[2]

In order to unpack fundamental and overarching elements of world-class cultures, we would be well served to first define what the term *culture* actually means. *Culture* most often refers to the social customs and practices of a particular group of people, either in the group's current state or from a historical perspective (nations/empires, races, belief systems, etc.). Many of us likely recall learning about various types of cultures in school. There is even a branch of anthropology, known as social anthropology, which is specifically focused on the study of human societies and their development.

For the purpose of our journey together, the scope of this book has been narrowed considerably within the framework of business or marketplace culture. With this distinction in mind, here is my definition of *corporate culture*, which I have extrapolated from years of personal experience and discovery: *corporate culture* is the collective beliefs and norms of an organization that drive predictable actions and related outcomes.

I also like the way Doug Claffey, co-founder of market research firm Energage, talks about the concept of organizational culture. Though you may not have heard of Energage, you will likely be familiar with the hundreds of Top Workplaces awards programs the firm represents annually across the country. Claffey and his team know something about culture and employee engagement, having surveyed more than twenty million individuals across fifty-eight thousand organizations since the company's inception in 2006. In my prior interview with Claffey in early 2020, he described culture as "a set of behaviors and values that organizations consistently exhibit, particularly when leadership is not in the room." In other words, corporate culture is about abiding by a collection of instilled principles, regardless of the situation and who might or might not be watching.[3]

Every organization has a culture, whether by default or deliberate design and whether anyone internally has taken the time to verbalize it or not. It is also important to note that many toxic cultures experience great financial success, at least for a while. I would argue that in these scenarios, the success is either short lived or something that is occurring in spite of the toxicity. Cautionary tales of once "great" companies like Enron and Lehman Brothers dot the landscape of shameful businesses past.

A growing body of research quantifying the economic benefits of a focused approach to culture is readily available to us, and it paints a compelling and largely irrefutable picture of highly competitive differentiation. For instance, in a study conducted as part of their groundbreaking book *Corporate Culture and Performance*, Harvard Business School professors John Kotter and James Heskett found that companies with strong cultures and a well-defined purpose achieved four times the revenue growth of those without strong cultures. In addition, firms with a proven culture realized a twelve-times advantage in stock price.[4] A commitment to becoming exceptional is not just the socially responsible thing to do. It's also the *financially* responsible thing to do!

The following pages will serve as a road map for irresistibility, a pathway to exceptional cultures. We will cover what it takes to construct a championship-level business, starting with an overview of common perspectives regarding work. Next, we will turn our attention to the role of the CEO and senior leadership to properly set a "tone from the top" that continuously articulates and models your company's purpose and core values. As we continue together on the pathway to purpose, we'll discover ways to tap into the power of middle management: those serving on the front lines every day and charged with molding their teams into a cohesive unit of highly engaged and inspired corporate athletes. Finally, we will explore key practices for employee acquisition, performance management, learning and development, and recognition and accountability.

Buckle up, and get ready for some counterintuitive twists and turns along the way. The culture transformation journey, should you decide to embark upon it, will be long and challenging - and unlike conventional corporate projects and initiatives, this race has no finish line. The pathway to purpose is not for the faint of heart. It is not for companies that are perfectly content with running with the pack or even those that aspire to become better than average. This is about striving to be the best of the best. It is about inspiring your team of corporate athletes to join forces in accomplishing something greater together than could ever be accomplished alone.

When executed properly, your company will unquestionably achieve the most commonly sought-after business outcomes: market share, growth, and profitability, to name a few. But even more importantly, you will gain a deeper appreciation for living out your noble purpose on a daily basis. And that, my friends, will make the journey well worth the sacrifice. Now, let's get started!

He who has a "why" to live can bear almost any "how."
—Friedrich Nietzsche

Chapter 1

SEEING: INFUSE COMMON PURPOSE

"I 'm heading south for the winter!" Those were the words I exclaimed to my parents on that momentous August afternoon. Fresh out of college, I had just been offered a job working in the front office for the Orlando Magic NBA basketball team. You would have thought I had won the lottery.

It was 1992, and the fledgling basketball franchise was entering its fourth year of existence. The team had yet to record a winning record, but the upcoming season brought with it some big hopes for future success. Now, when I say *big*, I mean it literally, in the form of number-one draft pick Shaquille O'Neal! At just over seven feet tall and well over three hundred pounds, Shaq was projected to be a once-in-a-generation talent on the court.

But I'm getting ahead of myself here. Regarding my pending job with the Magic, it wasn't exactly a real job, at least not in the traditional sense. For the next nine months, I would serve in the role of *unpaid* intern, working upwards of seventy hours per week in the organization's public relations department. As one might expect from an internship gig, the work was far from high profile. My time was largely spent sloughing around boxes of media guides, coordinating game credential requests, compiling press packets, and handling a host of other nondescript tasks. Meanwhile, on non-game days I would make my way to the nearby Quincy's Steakhouse where I moonlighted as a waiter and busboy. Whew. I get exhausted just thinking about those early days!

Here is the interesting thing, though. I wouldn't trade that stage of my career for any amount of money or prestige. Despite the fatigue and unsung nature of the work, I absolutely loved jumping out of bed every day. Even for us interns, it became apparent right away that we were on the ride of a lifetime!

The arrival of Shaquille to Central Florida was like catching lightning in a bottle. No one had ever witnessed anything like "the diesel" in modern-day sports – an astounding blend of size, strength, explosiveness, and child-like exuberance that was an amazing sight to behold. He was a one-man wrecking crew, shattering backboards and "posterizing" opponents wherever he played. All of us fortunate enough to watch practice on that first day of training camp knew that Shaq was even better than advertised...*way better.*

Thanks to the presence of Shaquille and a gradual infusion of additional talent like Penny Hardaway and Horace Grant, the Orlando Magic would become the hottest ticket in town – sorry Disney World and Universal Studios! Adoring fans, media and A-level celebrities from far and wide descended on O-town to see the Magic play up close and personal. The perennial underdog had become league top dog, and the team would remain elite until Shaq's unexpected departure to the LA Lakers several years later.

Following that initial season, I was blessed to transition from unpaid intern to bona fide team member, and I would spend the next six years with the Magic in numerous special project and service excellence roles. During this time, the team would become a force to be reckoned with, culminating in a trip to the NBA Finals in 1995. I'm happy to say we flourished off the court too, earning a reputation as one of the most admired sports organizations in the world in terms of season ticket holder loyalty, community service impact, and employee engagement.

It is in this unique environment that my fascination with corporate culture was initially formed. For the first time, I discovered there can (and should) be more to our work than the work itself, and that true magic lies at the intersection of passion and purpose. This realization would become a guiding principle for how I approached future career opportunities, and it shaped my life mission to help others pursue and design their own cultures of distinction.

Determine What Matters

If you are reading this book, chances are good that you are serious about making your life count. You want to look back someday and know that you ran the full race, fought the good fight, and fulfilled your destiny. And you want to have made a tangible difference, not just in the lives of your family and friends, but in the realm of *work*, too.

For far too many people, work is a daily grind which leads to significant discontent and regret. A recent Gallup workplace engagement study reveals that only 35 percent of US workers are *engaged*, meaning they are highly enthusiastic about and committed to their jobs and workplace. Meanwhile, the percentage of *actively disengaged* workers—those who are miserable at work and spread their unhappiness to their colleagues—is a dismal 13 percent. The remaining 52 percent of workers are in the *not-engaged* category, which indicates they are psychologically unattached to their work and organization.[1] The not-engaged will devote ample time to perform the basic requirements of the job, but they will withhold any discretionary passion or effort.

> When you receive payment after supplying the need of a
> client, a customer, or your boss…that money is testament
> to your having pleased another human being.
> —Dave Ramsey

In 2009, sales and organizational culture expert Lisa McLeod was hired by a pharmaceutical company to evaluate the effectiveness of their sales team. A primary objective of the effort was to identify the characteristics or attributes separating top performers from everyone else.

The research was conducted as a blind study to ensure complete project objectivity, meaning McLeod and her team were not informed in advance who the top sales performers were. Sales-rep interactions with physicians and other providers were closely observed, and a host of in-depth interviews were conducted by McLeod to better understand team-member backgrounds and related work habits. Call reports and other typical sales documentation were also studied, all in search of the specific ingredients common to the best of the best.

What Lisa McLeod and her lieutenants ultimately discovered should serve as a wake-up call for those who view their work as a daily grind instead of a sacred calling. Here is part of the story in McLeod's own words:

Then came the day that changed everything.

Near the end of the study, I was wrapping up a ride along with a rep from Phoenix, Arizona. After two days of working with this rep, I knew she was exceptional. I've observed thousands of sales calls, and she checked all the boxes. She asked great questions, she knew the science of her products backwards and forwards, she had a well-crafted call plan, and she was also flexible in the moment.

More than that, there was a certain magic about her interactions with customers that transcended the product, even the subject. She was more dialed in, more authentic and more emotionally engaged. As a result, the physicians and providers she spoke with became more emotionally engaged as well.

So, in our last few minutes together, I decided to ask her a question that wasn't on our standard list of interview questions.

I asked, "What do you think about when you go on sales calls?"

She told me a story I'll never forget.

She said, "I don't tell this to many people, but the truth is I always think about this one particular patient. One day, a few years ago, when I had just started with this company,

I was standing in a doctor's office waiting to speak to the doctor.

This little old lady came up to me and said, 'Excuse me Miss., do you work for that drug company?' I looked down at her and said, 'Yes ma'am, I do.' The little old lady looked up at me and said 'I just want to thank you. I want to thank you for giving me my life back. Prior to taking this drug, I couldn't go anywhere, I couldn't do anything. But now I can get on a plane, I can visit my grandkids, and I can get down on the floor and play with them. So thank you for giving me my life back.'"

The rep started to get emotional as she was telling me the story, and I found myself getting emotional as well. She concluded, "That's my purpose. I think about her every single day."

I got out of the car, schlepped through the airport, and boarded the long flight home. With plenty of time to think, I kept pondering it over and over in my head. Was this—this thing I now call Noble Purpose—the differentiator we had all been looking for?

I got back to my office and poured over the interview notes looking for reps who alluded to a sense of higher purpose...I found five total reps who alluded to it.

At the end of the study our client asked us, who do you think the top performers are. I said, "I think it's these five." I was 100% right. And the rep who told me the story about the grandmother was the top performing salesperson in the country for 3 years in a row.[2]

If work truly has the potential to be impactful and rewarding, why do we so often experience it in such negative ways? What keeps us from finding true purpose in our professions? Let's take some time now to explore some common explanations.

Dodging Pain at the Expense of Purpose

In the classic book *Man's Search for Meaning*, psychiatrist Victor Frankl shares his harrowing account of imprisonment and torture in a Nazi concentration camp during World War II. Frankl endured extreme physical and psychological pain during his three years of confinement and largely credits his survival on a belief that all aspects of life, both good and bad, can be ascribed greater meaning. Following his release, Frankl introduced the concept of logotherapy (from the Greek word *logos*, meaning "reason" or "principle"), which surmises that our chief motivation as humans is not to gain pleasure or to avoid pain but to find true purpose in life.[3]

Every significant and enduring accomplishment along life's journey is accompanied by some combination of fear, uncertainty, worry, discomfort, and/or pain. Achieving anything on a grand scale requires a willingness to extend beyond our comfort zone and work in a way that runs contrary to our human proclivity to chase comfort and contentment. As much as our natural self seeks to avoid the bumps and bruises along the way, they are a prerequisite to a fulfilled life—not an easy life, mind you, but one that taps into the very purpose for which we were designed. Of course, this reality can be easily overlooked at times, particularly when we experience work as just a means to an end…"I work to live," as opposed to something of immeasurable, inherent value…"I live to work."

Failing to Properly Assess Our Perceptions of Work

You may have heard the parable of the three stonecutters. Many years ago, a man was traveling a long distance by foot and came across three people in a field breaking large stones into pieces. He asked the first stonecutter what he was doing, to which the man rolled his eyes and in an exasperated tone said, "I'm breaking up stones and throwing them in a pile. I hate this job, and I cannot wait until quitting time to go home and rest." The visitor proceeded a bit farther and asked the second person the same question. This gentleman wiped his brow and responded, "I'm cutting these stones so that they can be made into a wall. It is really hard work, but it's OK, I suppose. I am thankful to make a decent wage that allows me to put food on my family's table." Finally, the traveler asked the third person what he was up to. The man stopped for a moment, backing up slightly to admire his work, and with a huge smile on his face said, "I'm making a living, but I'm also making a difference. These stones are being used to form a series of huge walls, and the walls will eventually be constructed into a beautiful cathedral to be enjoyed by people for generations to come. I love my job!"

In the stonecutter parable, we observe three people doing the exact same job, but they see their work in very different contexts. The first views his occupation as a means of survival. He's grinding through a miserable existence day after day for no other reason than to eke out enough to make ends meet. It is all about survival. No doubt, this gentleman would quit in a heartbeat if he had the financial means to do so. Sadly enough, countless numbers of people on the planet go to work every day and approach their jobs in much the same way. How about you? Can you personally identify with this highly depressing state of being? I was there at one point in my own career, and it is an extremely dark place to be.

I suspect the second stonecutter represents how the vast majority of us perceive our work at any given time. While we may not despise our jobs, our work does not necessarily inspire us in a truly meaningful way, either. Work is transactional in this example, but it does not rise to the level of being transformational.

The final stonecutter has a radically different perspective on his work. He *loves* his job, which suggests work has evolved into more of a *want to* than a *have to*. What's more, he believes the toils of his labor today will make a difference in the lives of those around him tomorrow. This individual is legacy building, and he understands he is connected to an effort that is much bigger than himself. Work has meaning and purpose. It does not mean every day is perfect and that there are not problems and major obstacles facing us on a regular basis. And it certainly doesn't mean that we don't experience pain and failure and exhaustion and fear along the way. But for those of us who have experienced jobs we love, it's about getting out of bed every day on a mission to fully engage in what we were created to do.

Unfortunately, the perspective of work for so many people in the world rarely, if ever, rises to the level of deeper purpose. There is no passion relative to contributing to a greater good and no sense of accomplishment on the other side of another honest day's work. Sadly enough, many of us have given up any real hope that our current job situation could ever change for the better. But as we can infer from this account and my opening example with the Magic, we have a *choice* in the matter. We have the freedom to choose how we interpret the environment around us, including our work environment. Regardless of our past employment or our current job status, we have the ability to control our thoughts and feelings. And for those of us blessed to live in a capitalistic society, we can freely pursue new opportunities when we feel our work does not properly align with our purpose.

Enduring Overbearing Bosses

Mental constructs certainly play a major role in our perceptions of a given situation, and they are undoubtedly critical to the ways in which we experience the world. Too many managers still tend to rule their subordinates with an iron fist, drawing upon command-and-control tactics in ill-advised psychological efforts to get the job done no matter how many body bags they leave on the way. I experienced this type of environment firsthand in the earlier days of my career. As part of a bizarre senior-leadership-meeting ritual, our CEO would randomly select one of us seated around the boardroom table each morning to verbally disparage and humiliate in front of our peers. It was not uncommon for these "dress-down" sessions to go on for fifteen to twenty minutes, particularly for my divisional counterparts in sales and operations. But sadly, none of us was fully exempt from the psychological beatings.

For a time, these types of misguided individuals may get the results they are seeking, but their relentless negativity will always incite toxic cultures with excessive turnover and plunging employee engagement. The popular quotation regarding the underlying motivation driving employee defections certainly rings true. "People don't generally quit their jobs. They quit their bosses."

A bit later in this book, we will explore the ideal role of bosses in significant detail but suffice it to say that leaders cannot mandate that anyone follow them. The modern-day company dictator may compel subordinates into submission through idle threats and intimidation, but they will never capture their passion and creativity through brute force. Alas, might does *not* make right.

Succumbing to Possession Obsession

For many people, particularly in the West, the fruits of our work fuel an insatiable desire for stuff. We find short-term pleasure and satisfaction in the acquisition of new things. A materialistic thirst for what society tells us are the latest and greatest *must-haves* can devolve into a possession obsession. Consider your cousin Tina, who camps out in the Apple store parking lot for two solid days prior to every new iPhone model launch. Or how about your neighbor Joseph, who insists on trading in his perfectly good luxury vehicle every six months for the upgraded version that just rolled off the factory floor?

A closer evaluation reveals we are all susceptible to sometimes slipping into *possession obsession*. For instance, I am a sucker for anything that has a North Carolina Tarheel logo slapped on it. No doubt you would be shocked to learn how much I spend on Tarheel paraphernalia every year!

Our materialistic appetites are frequently nourished by way of our vocations. "If I just work a little harder," we tell ourselves, "I'll finally be able to buy that new [fill in the blank], And *then* I'll truly be fulfilled." But as the old cliché goes, "You can't take your stuff with you."

You'll also never see a U-Haul being pulled by a hearse!

Prioritizing Profit over People

Fiscal pressures to perform in the immediate here and now have never been stronger in business, particularly for publicly traded entities. By failing to hit their quarterly earnings guidance, senior decision makers know their stock prices (and reputation) are likely to take a nosedive, even if the short-term miss is ultimately in the longer-term best interest of the company.

Not surprisingly, history is replete with cases where executives succumb to earnings pressures by sabotaging the future viability of the very businesses they have been entrusted to safeguard—think Enron, Volkswagen, Wells Fargo, etc. Alas, a longer-term focus on staff development does not typically align with *short-term* investor demands. Consider how stock prices are likely to *spike* following an organizational announcement regarding large-scale employee layoffs and conversely *dip* after notifying the public of a pending investment in a proven employee-training program.

Financial performance is king and rightfully so. Miss your quarterly earnings too many times, and your business will shrivel and die, no matter how well you treat your employees and customer base! But here is the big idea. Do not sacrifice stakeholder equity at the feet of shareholder demands. Your people make your performance possible. Put your people first, and financial prosperity will follow. This principle is equally true in both the public and private realms.

Consider whether the pursuits you might be delaying or putting off completely are the same ones that will bring you financial and cultural prosperity over the long term. A deliberate and thoughtful strategy focused on the execution of basic building blocks—such as professional development activities, customer feedback systems, research-and-development efforts, and timely infrastructure enhancements—will position your company for sustained excellence.

True character is revealed in the choices a human
being makes under pressure. The greater the pressure,
the deeper the revelation, the truer the choice to the
character's essential nature.
—Robert McKee

Falling Prey to the Work/Life-Balance Myth

The notion of work/life balance sounds great in theory but has proven to be largely unattainable in actual practice. Remember the popular and somewhat controversial Enjoli perfume commercial in the 1980s—the one with the unflappable female actor who croons so convincingly, "I can bring home the bacon. Fry it up in a pan. And never, ever let you forget you're a man!" In other words, it represents an almost idealistic naiveté, where one enjoys total control over time and space, seamlessly navigating the human experience without encountering any bumps or bruises along the way.

The myth of attaining some picture-perfect work/life equilibrium has risen to even greater prominence in recent years. It loves to whisper in our ear that we can (and should) be 100 percent dedicated to our work while simultaneously being fully committed to everything else (health, family, social relationships, church, community service, etc.). Anything less than perfect balance means we are at best a poor manager of time and at worst a pathetic loser. With the advent of the internet into mainstream America in the early 1990s and the introduction of smartphones shortly thereafter, the lines of demarcation between the traditional workplace and our personal lives are even more blurred.

Similarly, the practice of teleworking has become an increasingly popular work arrangement in recent years, driven in large part by savings accrued from reduced office space and related operating expenses. At the same time, research reveals that providing employees the opportunity to work from home *can* lead to improved employee engagement levels and even higher job productivity. When you take into consideration advanced collaboration tools like Zoom and Microsoft Teams, in combination with a massive wave of stay-at-home workers spurred by the COVID-19 pandemic, it is clear that remote working is here to stay.

All of this sounds well and good, but there are potential negative consequences resulting from prolonged periods of teleworking. It is a bizarre scenario where amazing technologies connect us to the world like never before yet actually leave us feeling alone and *disconnected* from coworkers. Unprecedented virtual connectivity can also lead to anxiety and burnout as we struggle to ascertain where work actually ends and leisure begins.

In today's world, we want our professional lives to matter in the same way we want our personal lives to matter. True balance is elusive, but work/life *integration* is a much more practical paradigm. With work/life integration, we concede the impossibility of perfect equilibrium, and we give ourselves permission to lean into one area over another depending on the situation. So, for example, if you are heading up a major IT upgrade that is set to roll out in two weeks, it would be wise to free up lots of early morning and late evening time, just in case any problems arise (which they will). Likewise, don't forget to carve out plenty of calendar space for your daughter's annual dance recital next Thursday afternoon, particularly after the mess you got yourself into last year when the recital ran forty-five minutes late and you had to bail to take a scheduled client call!

Work/life integration is also quite helpful when it comes to the way we approach specific seasons of life. My early post collegiate years were heavily focused on building my career, while the pendulum swung toward the needs of my family following the birth of our first child. More than anything, integration is about making sure whatever you are focused on (personal or professional) is in direct alignment with your overarching life purpose.

Next Steps on the Pathway-to-Purpose Journey

→ **Describe what the following statement means to you:** "The most important thing about you is who you are, not what you do."

→ **Share your life purpose with a person you trust.** If you don't have a personal purpose statement, take time today to develop one. Have someone confirm that your purpose reflects who you are at your very best. Keep refining until the statement accurately articulates the difference you were designed to make in the world.

→ **Consult with your key leaders to identify any *actively disengaged* employees.** Discuss how these individuals are impacting your workplace culture. What steps will be necessary to either move them up or out of the organization?

→ **Spend dedicated time with your leadership team discussing work/life integration.** What might this concept look like in actual practice within your organization?

→ **Review the tale of the three stonecutters.** Which of the characters depicted in the story are most like you when it comes to your personal view of work? Ask a trusted work confidante to provide you with their unvarnished point of view. Commit to personally addressing any negative differences of opinion.

Chapter 2

LEADING: CLEAR THE PATH

Legend has it that on the heels of a long and treacherous journey across the Atlantic Ocean in 1519, Spanish conquistador Hernán Cortés, in his conquest to capture the Aztec Empire, did something very unexpected prior to engaging the enemy. Some might even argue he had completely lost his mind. With absolute certainty, Cortés commanded his six hundred soldiers to "burn the boats!"[1] Though certainly a highly risky (and arguably reckless) move, Cortés drew a hard line in the sand that day, with crystal-clear implications: either win the ensuing battle, or die trying. There would be nowhere to run and nowhere to hide. Needless to say, the act of destroying their only means of escape had the intended impact, and the highly motivated Spanish contingent emerged victorious.

This military mission underscores the importance of senior leadership in any endeavor, including the world of business. The courage and conviction of the vital few set the cultural tone for the larger enterprise. Great corporate cultures are fundamentally seeded, cultivated, and harvested within the C-suite. Safety nets and backdoor escape routes can protect us from potential short-term pain and suffering, but they also tend to water down the focus, effort, and commitment we invest into a passionate cause. If you want to be exceptional, dispose of plan B when it comes to remaining true to your organizational culture. No hedging your bets. No turning back when things get tough. As famous boxer turned philosopher Mike Tyson once said, "Everyone has a plan until they get punched in the mouth!" Do not deviate from the bigger picture. Burn the boats!

Note that I am not advocating you resist altering company goals or strategic direction when market changes or customer requirements dictate that you should. Stubbornly standing pat in such cases poignantly illustrates the often-cited definition of *insanity*, which is "doing the same things you've always done and expecting different results." What you *do not* want to deviate from, however, are the fundamental beliefs and guiding principles that make your organizational DNA uniquely different from your competitors. So stick to your guns on the important stuff, but remain nimble with regard to evolving processes, patterns, and strategies. As a person of great influence within your enterprise, ask yourself this important question:

Am I committed, or am I just interested?
—Ken Blanchard

It is not impossible to drive a culture of excellence without top-down support, but rest assured it will not come easily. The path becomes significantly less burdensome when the CEO (a.k.a. "chief evangelist officer") and senior leaders serve as primary architects and catalysts for fueling cultural excellence. By virtue of their position, senior leaders are ultimately accountable for the humanity of the organization. While they certainly assume oversight for the success of the business, they also bear great responsibility for the well-being of their workforce, laying the groundwork for personal engagement and prosperity. Think about it: every individual under a leader's care is someone's son or daughter and should be treated with great care and dignity. Your team is made up of real people with real hopes and aspirations, real strengths and fears, and a real desire to make a difference in the world.

Consider the most venerated corporate cultures of our day. Behind each one, you will find an executive leader (past or present) who boldly established the culture by regularly communicating a well-defined purpose and vision across the enterprise and by personally modeling expected behaviors with every interaction. Leadership requires a willingness to stay true to a larger cause, even when doing so might seem uncertain or frightening in the moment.

For greater context, let's play a quick game of "name the founding CEO" from several highly acclaimed cultural icons.

Organization	Founding CEO
Disney	Walt Disney
Spanx	Sara Blakely
Ritz-Carlton	Horst Schulze
Chick-fil-A	Truett Cathy
Starbucks	Howard Schultz
Apple	Steve Jobs

You are likely familiar with each of the companies listed above and at least a majority of the individuals that made them household names. In their respective tenures as commander-in-chief, each leader checked all the requisite boxes necessary for developing workplaces of distinction. Over the following pages, we will take a closer look at some of these remarkable leaders and how they built such iconic cultures. But first, let's revisit the essential role of purpose.

Begin with Why

The most effective way to tap into the best of your workforce is to invite them to participate in the larger organizational cause. Purpose is the tip of the spear for developing irresistible cultures. Even your most capable employees need a clearly defined purpose—a North Star to ensure their time and talents are focused strategically on pushing themselves and the organization forward. Resist the temptation to confine your purpose to a select group of senior leaders. Instead, grant everyone the opportunity to embrace who your company is when it is performing at its collective best.

You can't start a fire without a spark, and you can't start a revolution without a unified cause.

As we discussed in chapter 1, purpose speaks to our reason for being. It is the very essence of our existence. It's the emotionally charged motivation behind *why* we do the things we do. Without a clearly defined why, life lacks meaning and passion. Aristotle believed that humans are teleological beings, meaning that above all else, we are driven to discover our true calling, our unique purpose. In light of this drive, we feel most happy and in control when we have a clear picture of what we are moving toward each day.

Purpose applies in the same way to our careers. Without it, our work becomes more about making a living and less about making a difference. Vision statements, core values, competencies, underlying goals, and the like are all very important, but the need for a well-articulated, fully deployed, enterprise-wide purpose should eclipse everything else in order of priority. Here is why: purpose connects our logical minds with our emotional hearts, regardless of the confluence of circumstances that may exist at any particular moment in time. Corporate vision and goals will change as necessary over time, but a corporate purpose is unwavering. It stands the test of time. Just as individuals yearn for personal meaning, enterprises thrive when leadership brings forth a global purpose that inspires others to join in a cause far greater than themselves.

The following excerpt from a 1960 speech given by Hewlett-Packard co-founder, David Packard, further highlights the predominant role of organizational purpose:

> I want to discuss why a company exists in the first place...I think many people assume, wrongly, that a company exists simply to make money. While this is an important result of a company's existence, we have to go deeper and find the real reasons for our being...Purpose (which should last at least 100 years) should not be confused with specific goals or business strategies (which should change many times in 100 years). Whereas you might achieve a goal or complete a strategy, you cannot fulfill a purpose; it's like a guiding star on the horizon—forever pursued but never reached. Yet although purpose itself does not change, it does inspire

change. The very fact that purpose can never be fully realized means that an organization can never stop stimulating change and progress.[2]

According to authors Sally Blount and Paul Leinwand, in a December 2019 *Harvard Business Review* article entitled "Why Are We Here?," purpose statements should always speak to the reason your company exists and why your customers should care. Though seemingly obvious on the surface, it can often be overlooked that the satisfaction and loyalty of your customers fuels your organization's long-term viability. A shared purpose serves as a written promise to your end users. It is a pledge on behalf of a highly motivated workforce to keep customers at the forefront of every organizational decision and strategy. A purpose statement that fails to put the customer first is one destined for marginal impact.[3]

At the time our leadership team was developing a purpose statement at Atlantic Capital Bank, we could have easily stated we were in business to "become the most profitable (or most respected, or largest, etc.) commercial bank in the Southeast." However, this would have been more of a vision statement, signifying what we aspired to achieve instead of describing why it should be important to our teammates and our clients. Chances are that without a meaningful purpose statement, our team members would not be inspired today to join the bigger cause, and our customers would fail to see that our intentions are honorable and pure.

After significant time and reflection, we landed on a simple but inspiring phrase to represent our corporate purpose. At Atlantic Capital, "we fuel client prosperity." We came to work every day not just for a paycheck but to help power the unique dreams and aspirations of our clients. For us, it was not just about the money. It was also about the meaning.

As Blount and Leinwand point out, it is hard to envision employees bringing the best version of themselves to work every day if they do not understand the essence of your organizational purpose and the unique role everyone plays in bringing the purpose to life. Sadly, a 2019 employee study conducted by Strategy&, an affiliate of PwC, revealed that only 28 percent of respondents feel connected to their organization's purpose, and just 39 percent said they clearly see the value they create. A mere 22 percent indicated they believe their jobs allow them to fully leverage their strengths.[4]

Simply asking your people to memorize a purpose statement is not enough to drive substantive change. Positioning purpose as a corporate slogan or motto also greatly misses the mark. Organizational purpose is a pathway to connecting the hearts and minds of your workforce. It requires leaders who embrace the bigger picture and are committed to helping their teams connect the dots to a better way. We will spend more focused time in the next chapter exploring ways that leadership can inspire others to bring their discretionary energy to work every day, but for now, remember that everything rises and falls with you.

Following are purpose statements from the companies we listed earlier. Look and ask yourself whether each statement accurately reflects the unique persona of the founding executive leader and organization it represents. Then read on to learn how the creators of Chick-fil-A and Ritz-Carlton ingrained purpose into their companies.

Organization	Founding CEO	Purpose Statement
Disney	Walt Disney	To create happiness by providing the finest in entertainment for people of all ages, everywhere
Spanx	Sara Blakely	To invent and enhance products that promote comfort and confidence in women
Ritz-Carlton	Horst Schulze	To provide the finest personal service and facilities for our guests
Chick-fil-A	Truett Cathy	To glorify God by being a faithful steward of all that is entrusted to us
Starbucks	Howard Schultz	To inspire and nurture the human spirit—one person, one cup, and one neighborhood at a time
Apple	Steve Jobs	To make a contribution to the world by making tools for the mind that advance humankind

Eat Mor Chikin

I recently visited a local Chick-fil-A near my home office for a quick bite to eat and was totally unsurprised to encounter a line at least thirty cars deep in the drive-through plus a parking lot filled to absolute capacity. Despite the high business volume, the place ran like a well-oiled machine, as employees from both inside and outside the establishment cheerfully greeted guests, patiently took guest orders, and served them up with uncanny speed and accuracy. Team members and customers alike were content to play their designated roles in the transaction...to serve and to be served.

I mention that I was not surprised because it seems that pretty much *every* Chick-fil-A is packed around lunch or dinnertime on any given day. What I did find particularly intriguing, however, was the contrasting scene I observed directly across the street at a McDonald's location: a grand total of two cars in the drive-through and six vehicles parked in the lot! And I feel pretty confident that at least a few of the parked cars belonged to Mickey D's employees.

So what gives here? The meteoric rise of Chick-fil-A as king of quick-service restaurants can be traced back to the extraordinary work ethic, determination, and faith of company founder Truett Cathy. His fascination with business formally began at just eight years old, selling bottles of Coca-Cola in his Eatonton, Georgia, neighborhood for a five-cent profit on every six bottles he sold.

Cathy launched his first restaurant, the Dwarf Grill, in suburban Atlanta in 1946. Ironically, hamburgers made up the bulk of sales for nearly two decades. In the early 1960s, Cathy began experimenting with the novel concept of a chicken sandwich, ultimately perfecting the right combination of seasonings and cooking technique. Chicken (or at least the chicken sandwich) would never be the same again!

In 1967, Cathy opened the first Chick-fil-A restaurant in Atlanta's Greenbriar Mall, to rave reviews. Fast-forward, and Chick-fil-A has since grown to more than two thousand locations and nearly twenty-five thousand employees in the United States alone. Key Chick-fil-A financial metrics are equally impressive, including an astounding fifty-one consecutive years of revenue growth and a whopping $10 billion in 2018 sales. What's more, the company is easily the most successful fast-food chain in America on a per-unit basis. The QSR 50, a ranking of the top fifty quick-service and fast-casual restaurant companies by US system-wide sales, reveals that per-unit sales for behemoth McDonalds was approximately $2.7 million in 2018 compared to *$4.1 million* for Chick-fil-A. This is a remarkable performance, particularly taking into account that Chick-fil-A is only open six days a week![5]

Cathy followed a business model that would ensure a consistent experience across every restaurant, particularly with regard to customer service, employee behaviors, and operational quality. More than anything, he realized early on that the key to large-scale growth would depend on the selection of great people. As Cathy himself noted, "We concentrate on people. And I know sometimes the stock companies concentrate on the bottom line. We should forget about the bottom line. It is important that we do things right and do things right long enough that you will receive the rewards that you were looking for."[6]

Truett Cathy, who passed away in 2014 at the age of ninety-three, never deviated from his North Star principles over a sixty-five-year career in the restaurant industry. He viewed his work as a sacred opportunity to honor God and to serve every person and team member that enters a Chick-fil-A restaurant. His story proves that it is possible to hold true to strong values in both business and life.

> Learn to love your work, and you'll never
> have to "work" again.
> —Truett Cathy

Move Heaven and Earth

Ritz-Carlton founder and former CEO Horst Schulze was a pioneer in the service and hospitality industry. He was born in a small German village in the Mosel region and left home at fourteen to begin work as a busboy. Schulze notes, "I knew I wanted to be in hotels [starting] at the age of 11.

My parents finally agreed to let me leave and I've lived in hotels ever since."[7] In August of 1983, Schulze was hired by businessman William B. Johnson to form the present-day version of Ritz-Carlton. He would remain with the company until his departure in 2001.

As a regional performance improvement leader with Ritz, I had the opportunity to interact with Schulze on numerous occasions and observe him relentlessly drive the culture forward. From Schulze's vantage point, you *manage* processes, and you *lead* people. In Schulze's world, second place was just not good enough. Mediocrity was unacceptable.

And it showed in the rise of Ritz-Carlton as the premier player in the luxury hotel market. Under Schulze's direction and influence, the company would receive an unprecedented two Malcolm Baldrige National Quality Awards, numerous travel leisure awards and the highest J. D. Power service score in the history of the rankings process. Schulze was the pied piper of service quality during his Ritz-Carlton days.

From the very beginning, competitive differentiation was not primarily a function of extravagant facilities in exotic locales, although Ritz-Carlton has historically delivered quite well on these fronts. Instead, the overwhelming advantage Ritz brings to the table can be found in the can-do mindset of an employee base that today boasts more than forty thousand employees. These are the ladies and gentlemen who bring the vision to life each and every day.

Hotel team members revered and beloved Schulze. We often spoke of moving heaven and earth to meet and exceed customer expectations. The essence of Ritz-Carlton as a cultural icon continues until this day and is a direct reflection of the excellence demanded by Horst Schulze and his senior leadership team. To Schulze, excellence was never a choice; it was a business mandate.

> We are superior to the competition because we hire
> employees who work in an environment of belonging
> and purpose. We foster a climate where the employee can
> deliver what the customer wants. You cannot deliver what
> the customer wants by controlling the employee.
> —Horst Schulze

As we have established, the pathway to irresistible cultures begins with uniting your organization around a formal purpose statement. To inspire your teammates to bring their very best to their jobs each day, they must recognize how their individual efforts contribute to the greater organizational good. You and your leadership team carry the responsibility for bringing the purpose to life, but there are other factors to keep in mind in establishing a cultural tone from the top.

Lead by Example

Walter Elias Disney was the brilliant founder and chief architect behind the Disney theme parks, the wildly popular destinations that are synonymous everywhere with childlike fun and adventure. After successfully launching Disneyland Park in Anaheim, California, in 1955, Walt Disney set his sights on the design of an even grander theme park on the East Coast. When he first arrived on the scene in Orlando, Florida, back in 1965, few would have conceived that the twenty-five thousand acres of orange groves Walt Disney purchased would eventually be transformed into the Magic Kingdom, a venue regularly billed as the most magical place on earth![8]

In many ways, Walt Disney set the stage for our modern-day corporate fascination with organizational culture. There is a mystique and aura about the Disney World experience that makes it refreshingly unique but at the same time remarkably consistent. Disney was a transformative visionary who understood the importance of his work on a grand scale. He also had a gift for inspiring others to join him on the journey, perfectly embodying the company purpose to "create happiness for people everywhere."

The Disney journey runs in sharp contrast to an intriguing tale about the expert archer who spent many years perfecting his craft. While traveling on foot to a distant village, the man came across the image of a bull's-eye painted on a large tree, with an arrow lodged directly in the tiny center circle. As he continued his expedition, he discovered numerous other bull's-eyes positioned on trees and even on the side of a barn wall. In each instance, an arrow was found sticking dead center in the smallest ring. The traveler was astonished, all the while growing increasingly determined to learn the identity of his new rival.

Through a series of unusual circumstances, he finally came face-to-face with the person responsible for all the perfect shots: a spunky and highly confident little ten-year-old girl. The traveler, now totally dumbfounded, demanded that the girl explain exactly how she could record a perfect bull's-eye with every shot. "It's really quite easy," she said with a growing excitement. "I draw my arrow tight in the bow. Then I point it very straight and let it go. And wherever it lands, I carefully draw a bullseye around it." While this story makes for a great laugh, it is not a recommended approach to lead your organization!

Walt Disney had a crystal-clear understanding of his calling in life, and he stayed true to his calling despite the many naysayers along the way. He did not just draw the picture of success in his mind's eye but put in the necessary work to become a master at his craft. He embraced his purpose and effectively modeled the way for generations of Disney team members to follow.

Of all the things I've done, the most vital is
coordinating those who work with me and aiming
their efforts at a certain goal.
—Walt Disney

Make Excellence a Forever Thing

As a key leader within your organization, one of the biggest minefields to avoid in architecting an irresistible workplace is allowing an employee mindset to fester in which an enterprise-wide culture rollout is viewed as just another program of the month. You know…March is Customer Appreciation Month, April is Eat Healthy Month, May is Practice Gratitude Month, and June—well, June is Change Our Company Culture Month!

We live in a microwave society where expected time horizons for results are constantly being constricted. Unable to find the obscure book you so desperately need for your daughter's middle school biology class at the local bookstore? No problem. Amazon can have it shipped to you within hours. Worried about that nasty stomach rash you discovered after work on Friday evening? No need to wait until Monday to see your doctor. There is a MinuteClinic located within five minutes of your house that gladly accepts your health insurance (and cash). Better yet, grab your iPad or smartphone and schedule to hold your appointment via telemedicine.

Unlike typical corporate projects and initiatives, the pathway to cultural excellence does not come with a predetermined end date. There is literally no finish line. If your company culture is to become a valid representation of all that you dreamed it could be, it must never take a back seat to anything.

Avoid Cultural Shortcuts

Designing an exceptional workplace should never be treated as a checkbox activity. Whenever you are dealing with human beings, there will always be rough edges to polish and opportunities to continuously innovate and improve. Culture transformation cannot be deployed or sustained by cutting corners.

Not too long ago, my daughter Elaina acquired an old desk from a friend of a friend, with the intent of using it in her new college apartment. The desk was attractive enough and appeared to be solidly built. Unfortunately, though, its current color (jet black) did not coordinate well with her existing bedroom furniture. "No problem," we thought. "We'll just paint over the old black paint with new white paint." Now to be very clear, DIY projects are not something the Lutz family (and me specifically) is particularly gifted at, but with a noble intention of saving time and a few bucks, we proceeded with our misguided confidence.

After applying a first coat of paint, it became painfully obvious that this was not going to be as easy of a task as we had hoped. The original dark color continued to show through just as clear as day. What's more, the new white paint began to bubble up and flake in numerous locations, particularly on the top flat desk surface. Applying a second and third coat of white paint didn't seem to help much either.

It turns out that in our rush to complete the project, we ignored a critical first step, a step that experienced painters would never dare leave out, regardless of perceived time constraints. We failed to apply an initial coat of primer, which forms a buffer of sorts for the new paint to stick to versus being absorbed and subjugated by the old paint.

The same principles apply when attempting to design outstanding cultures. If you do not properly prime first or attempt to skip steps in an ill-advised attempt to speed things up, the old will eventually just resurface. And the old will not sufficiently steer your company to a new and improved state.

Unfortunately, there is no magic pill to quickly unleash a company's purpose and core values into the hearts and minds of its employees. Just like a fine wine, an exceptional culture needs ample time to reach an optimal state. It requires an unfettered opportunity to further season and mature over the long haul.

Start with Your People
Think about it. From great cultures flow employees who view work as a "want to" instead of a "have to" proposition. Employees who understand that their work matters tend to contribute significantly more than those who are just there to earn a paycheck. In a recent research study conducted by the Tempkin Group, which evaluated the attributes people found most appealing in their jobs, 54.4 percent indicated an "inspiring mission" as the most important consideration. By contrast, just 27 percent chose "above-average pay" as the most important attribute.[8]

Employees who come to work every day knowing that they are contributing to the overall success of the organization will be more likely to serve their customers with a greater sense of passion and excellence. They will defend the company and their colleagues as if they were their own flesh and blood. And in these types of organizations, employees view the company brand as a symbol of their own identity.

Because of heightened levels of employee engagement, many customers will perceive a gap in the service experience provided by your company as compared to your competitors, though some may be unable to effectively verbalize the distinction at first. Loyal customers will increasingly emerge, rewarding your organization with their repeat business and unsolicited referrals to family and friends. The engagement cycle continues as your employees observe the positive impact they are having on customers. Not only are your customers less likely to depart in this type of environment but so, too, are your employees.

> The leaders of great organizations do not see people as a commodity to be managed to help grow the money. They see the money as the commodity to help grow their people.
> —Simon Sinek

Never Settle

Several months ago, I had the opportunity to hear an excellent keynote address at an Atlanta-based management symposium. Jeff Nischwitz is the founder of the Nischwitz Group, a consulting and coaching company focused on leadership development and helping businesses nurture high-performing teams. In reviewing his speaking bio prior to his talk, I noticed that Nischwitz referred to himself as a "snow globe shaker," a job title that was completely foreign to me. Of course, I could not wait to learn more.

It turns out that over the past several years, Nischwitz has become quite the snow globe aficionado, procuring them from most everywhere his travels take him. He also makes sure to have a favorite globe on stage with him for each of his speaking engagements, which was the case on this particular day.

Holding a particularly ornate globe showcasing a tiny, bustling town in some far away land, Nischwitz proceeded to do what any of us would do. He shook the globe, causing exquisite "snowflakes" to blanket every centimeter of the now wintery scene. The audience (me included) oohed and aahed while the snow transported us to a beautiful place bursting with excitement and boundless possibilities. But within a matter of seconds, the wonderland reverted to its normal state—still quite charming but lacking the earlier anticipation sparked by Nischwitz's initial globe shake.

Nischwitz went on to explain that the magic of the snow globe was akin to the cultural dynamic found in many of organizations he had worked with in the past. A scenario where well-intentioned senior leadership develop a campaign to "shake things up" within the company, to disrupt the status quo and design a culture that puts their people first and fuels a collective passion for excellence. Mission and vision statements are crafted, core values are dusted off, employee engagement committees are formed, and laminated cards are distributed highlighting cultural mandates to be followed going forward.

Likewise, company celebrations are held, and employees are supplied with numerous promotional items commemorating the new culture tagline. And everything goes great for a while, until organizational momentum begins to wane and the proverbial dust begins to *settle*, just like the snowflakes ultimately settled in the snow globe illustration.

Over time, the never-ending demands to meet the numbers, the daily whirlwind blowing team members in different strategic directions, and the competitive pressures causing dissension among the ranks can often lead companies to not only revert to their original state but at times erode organizational morale to a new low. Before you know it, disappointment and even a touch of cynicism begin to creep in after such a promising launch.

Don't settle for positioning your company to become less than it was meant to be. Don't settle for leading a good company instead of an exceptional one. Don't settle for failing to affect your customer's lives in a significant way. And don't look back someday and wish you had demanded more of yourself and your team.

Never settle. Burn the boats.

Next Steps on the Pathway-to-Purpose Journey

→ **Does your company have a formal purpose statement** that articulates the reason your business exists and why your customers should care? To what extent has your purpose been institutionalized across the entire enterprise? Beginning today, what steps will you take to further enliven your organizational purpose?

→ **Go back and review the "Begin with Why" section.** Spend time reflecting on the soul of your organization. What does your company bring to the world that is meaningful and unique?

→ **In what facets of your company culture do you feel leadership is "settling?"** For example, are you compromising cultural non-negotiables by recruiting highly competent people with little regard for your organizational core values? Are you cutting corners when it comes to delivering exceptional products or services to your customers? Are you inspiring a workforce to engage in something bigger than themselves, or just pushing them to get the work out no matter what it takes?

→ **Spend some time asking for feedback from some of your team members on the front line.** If your employees truly trust that you have their best interest in mind, you will be surprised at what you can learn! Take action today to address key areas of concern.

→ **What does the phrase "burn the boats" mean to you in the context of company culture?** As a person of significant organizational influence, what elements of the culture do you consider sacred? How can you ensure these elements do not erode over time? Think about what actions are necessary to inspire others to remain on purpose.

Chapter 3

BUILDING: CRAFT A LEGACY

The biblical parable of the wise and foolish builders illustrates the importance of constructing one's life from the ground up by starting with a firm foundation. The wise man built his house on rock; the foolish man built his on sand. When the winds blew, the house built on rock stood strong, while the one built on sand, though it might have previously looked fine on the outside, inevitably crumbled.[1]

The parable serves as an important reminder to focus our efforts on things that have long-term significance. It also speaks volumes to organizational leaders, who are entrusted with the competent and compassionate care of their respective teams. If human capital is truly the bedrock of an enterprise, then it is essential that our workforces be given a solid foundation on which to continuously grow and be inspired.

Nothing should take precedence over the collective pride and joy of our employees...not customers, nor shareholders, not new product launches or short-term profits. Dating back to Heskett, Sasser, and Schlesinger's research outlined in their 1997 best-selling book, *The Service Profit Chain*, we know that employees who are highly engaged provide customers with consistently greater service experiences, which ultimately leads to increased revenues and higher profitability.[2]

So, if we concede that high levels of employee engagement serve as powerful predictors of desired emotional and financial outcomes, then it is important to ask ourselves, "What are the core building blocks necessary to fuel exceptional workplace cultures? How do company influencers establish a firm foundation to ensure their organizations stand strong over

31

the long haul and don't crumble like a house of cards when the inevitable storms come calling?"

Over the following pages, we will evaluate the primary elements necessary to shape and fortify your culture and to prevent the organizational "settling" phenomenon described at the end of chapter 2. Just as civil engineers have for many years utilized steel reinforcing bars (known as rebar) as a means to strengthen concrete under tension, so, too, will adhering to these guidelines reinforce the durability and sustainability of your organization.

But before proceeding with our inventory of reinforcement strategies, let's validate the type of organizational culture we wish to design. In his best-selling book *The Advantage*, Patrick Lencioni discusses two very common types of companies, which he refers to as "hard" and "soft" businesses, neither of which by themselves is ideal. According to Lencioni, hard organizations are focused on *performance* and, taken to an extreme, contend that employees must be controlled to ensure productivity. Senior leaders seek to extract maximum effort from their teams with little regard for engagement or well-being. Hard organizations invoke lots of workplace stress and fuel high levels of mistrust and turnover. For hard organizations, these negatives are just the cost of doing business. We see few, if any, of the higher order "making a difference" views of work discussed in chapter 1 in this type of organization. Employees are interchangeable and easily replaceable...churn and burn. Lencioni argues that this mentality does not lead to sustainable success in business.

On the opposite end of the spectrum, soft organizations are all about maintaining the *dignity* of the people who work there. At an extreme, soft organizations coddle their people and accept them "as is" without regard for actual work performance. Accountability to meeting corporate goals and objectives is optional. Mediocrity or worse becomes the accepted norm within soft organizations. Ironically, despite all the focus placed on pampering team members, the workforce gradually becomes discouraged and disheartened. As with hard organizations, soft ones do not thrive over time.

Lencioni points out that the proper blend of performance and dignity fosters a culture of *inspiration*.[3] It is in the sweet spot between dignity and performance that team members are motivated to do their best work. Herein lies the pathway to purpose and work as it was designed to be. It is the cross-section between *what you do* and *why you do it.*

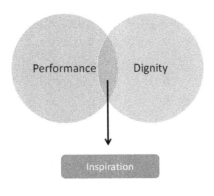

FIGURE 3.1

Now that we understand the endgame, let's explore essentials to avoid organizational settling. These are the foundational basics required to cultivate an ecosystem of true believers and to help your people find deeper meaning in their work. Each essential thrives under the influence and care of senior leadership.

Champion a Growth Mindset

Stanford University psychologist Carol Dweck is best known for her work on mindset and human potential. Her groundbreaking and best-selling book *Mindset* is a must read for anyone interested in personal growth and development. Dweck contends there are two basic ways that humans view themselves and their basic place in the world. People with a *fixed mindset* believe they are essentially a product of the talents and abilities that were endowed to them at birth, and there is therefore little reason to pursue any personal improvement efforts. The prospect of failure in the world of fixed mindset should be avoided at all costs because failing is a manifestation of your lot in life. If I fail at something, then that means I am a failure. In the psyche of someone with a fixed mindset, you are pretty much what you are, and no amount of effort or hard work is going to change this fact. You are left with no choice but to accept the hand that life has dealt to you—good or bad.

A second, more optimistic way people view themselves is referred to as *growth mindset*. Those with a growth mindset believe they are fully capable of improving, that individual success is not a result of winning the genetic sweepstakes but rather a by-product of hard work and sheer determination. Failure in the world of growth mindset is regarded as an opportunity to learn from your mistakes and to try again. Of course, each mindset has fundamental implications on the way we experience life, and each of us can at times unknowingly toggle between mindsets.

The good news is that by continuously challenging our thought patterns and underlying beliefs, we can condition our brains to more fully embrace the growth mindset and behave accordingly.

Dweck tells the story of a high school in Chicago with an unorthodox grading system. Students have to pass a certain number of classes to proceed to the next grade level, and if they do not pass a particular course, they receive a grade of "not yet." On the surface, the difference between a rubber-stamped "fail" and "not yet" might appear innocuous. After all, we're really just talking about basic semantics, right?

According to Dweck, the distinction between failure and "not yet" (i.e., fixed mindset and growth mindset) can literally be life altering. Listen to Dweck in her own words: "If you get a failing grade, you think, 'I'm nothing, I'm nowhere.' But if you get the grade 'not yet,' you understand that you're on a learning curve. It gives you a path into the future."[4]

"Not yet" implies that the game is still in play. Failing to achieve the results you hoped for does not mean your story is complete and disqualified from future revisions. It just means that you have not succeeded...*yet.* Sure, you might be experiencing a temporary roadblock, but you have not reached a dead end. You are not a finished product, and with resilience and perseverance, you can absolutely move closer to a desired outcome. You get to choose how you respond. "Not yet" means that success is potentially right around the corner. Today's setback is nothing more than a setup for a comeback. And who doesn't love a great comeback?

When confronted with the opportunity to change the direction of our lives for the better, it is only when we concede that the change is actually possible and within our control that we will proceed outside our comfort zone to make the change a reality. Only then will we willingly endure short-term pain for a long-term gain.

Jack Canfield, of Chicken Soup for the Soul fame, asserts there are only three things in life over which we have total control: the thoughts you think, the images you visualize, and the actions you take. And it all starts with our thinking.

> You become what you think about all day long.
> —Ralph Waldo Emerson

Research further points to an unmistakable connection between our beliefs and subsequent outcomes. Just 15 percent of individual/organizational success can be attributed to actual skills and knowledge, while the remaining 85 percent is tied directly to our belief systems around the concepts of unlimited potential (a belief in our ability to learn/grow) and ultimate responsibility (a belief in our ability to effect change). The things our society regularly dismisses as soft and unimportant are the same ones we so often neglect![5]

If we are to inspire our teams to become exceptional, we must foster a collective growth mindset, where learning from failure is encouraged, innovation is embraced, and stretching beyond our self-imposed limits is celebrated. The brain is constantly creating and destroying neural pathways, forming the thought and behavior patterns our brain uses to make decisions, choose actions, and present us to the outside world. The pathways that are used get stronger, while those that are underused grow weak and are eventually replaced. Exemplary companies thoughtfully and deliberately create learning and development environments that reinforce cultural mandates and fully leverage the malleability of our minds.

In many ways, we are the caretakers for the beliefs of our people. Once we truly believe our work has meaning and that we are hardwired for success, the road to an irresistible workplace becomes radically simplified.

Instill Confidence

Whereas many CEOs have built highly successful organizations centered on the importance of mutual trust, numerous others have paid a steep price for saying one thing and doing another. The infamous fall of former energy giant Enron at the turn of the century is an unfortunate illustration of how unscrupulous leadership within the highest levels of an organization can literally take a company and its workforce down. Under the watch of founder and CEO Kenneth Lay, Enron lost 99.7 percent of its more than $100 billion valuation by the end of November 2001.

Driven by an insatiable thirst to grow Enron revenues by any means necessary, Lay and his executive leaders used an array of accounting loopholes to hide billions of dollars in debt from numerous failed ventures. The influence of Enron's top brass ultimately permeated across an entire organization of more than twenty-nine thousand employees. As the old saying goes, "A fish rots from the head down."

After the scandal broke and the stock price plummeted, Enron shareholders filed a $40 billion lawsuit. A subsequent investigation by the US Securities and Exchange Commission, coupled with a failed purchase attempt by Enron competitor Dynegy, led to what was, at the time, the largest bankruptcy in American history. Not surprisingly, Lay and other Enron executives were later indicted for numerous charges and sentenced to prison.

Probably most ironic in this cautionary tale of greed and corruption is the list of core values Enron had etched in stone at their corporate headquarters in Houston, Texas: Communication, Respect, Integrity, and Excellence. Of particular significance is the company's articulation of the integrity value, which stated, "We work with customers and prospects openly, honestly, and sincerely."[6] With the benefit of hindsight nearly twenty years later, it is amazing to consider that Enron trumpeted integrity as a key point of marketplace differentiation. In reality, the shamed giant became a poster child for distrust and deception. It is a classic example of senior leadership failing to "walk the talk."

One of the truest tests of integrity is its blunt refusal
to be compromised.
—Chinua Achebe

Crafting cultures exemplified by trust is not just about keeping your promises. It is also about having the courage to be emotionally transparent, or what author Pat Lencioni refers to as "vulnerability-based trust." Vulnerability-based trust occurs when leaders "comfortably and quickly acknowledge, without provocation, their mistakes, weaknesses, failures, and needs for help. They also recognize the strengths of others, even when those strengths exceed their own." This deeper level of trust is a necessary ingredient for developing exceptional workplaces because it affords team members the impetus to authentically open up with one another about their faults and fears.

Leaders should be held to a higher standard when it comes to modeling this deeper-level trust. Hearing someone in authority openly apologize for a mistake, admit they do not have the answer, or share something emotionally relevant is a powerful thing. Your team will respect you for it, and they will ultimately be inspired to follow you into the fire.

Engendering an organizational culture of trust is not just the right thing to do. It has also been proven the financially prudent thing to do. The Great Place to Work Institute compiles the "100 Best Companies to Work For" in partnership with *Fortune*. Trust comprises two-thirds of the criteria on which companies are selected. It turns out that winning companies "beat the average annualized returns of the S&P 500 by a factor of three."[7]

Despite the clear need for trust and vulnerability within the business community, recent research conducted by the Society for Human Resources Management (SHRM) suggests we have plenty of room for improvement. In a recent SHRM study, employees were surveyed about forty-four key factors of job satisfaction. The survey item "trust between employees and senior management" ranked as the second-greatest contributor to job satisfaction among respondents (behind "respectful treatment of all employees"). Even more telling, there was a 28 percentage point differential between respondents who rated the trust question as very important and those who indicated they were very satisfied with this factor being demonstrated in their organization. Only "compensation/pay" recorded a higher differential between importance and satisfaction (35 percent).[8]

We will further explore the topic of trust, as well as key strategies to effectively foster trust, in the next chapter, but suffice it to say that the significance of trust within any enterprise cannot be overstated.

Connect the Dots

Several years ago, Wharton management professor and best-selling author Adam Grant studied a group of college students hired to solicit financial pledges from alumni on behalf of the university. As an experiment, Grant arranged for a recent graduate who had been awarded a scholarship funded through a similar solicitation effort to share his story with the students. The graduate gave a short talk about how the scholarship had positively affected his life and how grateful he was for the students' efforts. In the time frame immediately following the alumni testimonial, donations secured by the workers increased by a remarkable 171 percent. Interestingly, the surge occurred without any promise of additional compensation for increased production. Subsequent interviews with the students revealed that the alumni testimonial had inspired them to try harder and with greater passion. They had witnessed firsthand the greater purpose behind their work.[9]

When evaluating shared and enduring traits of the most admired companies on the planet, it is clear that irresistible cultures arise when employees are able to connect the dots between their unique job functions and the institution's overall purpose. Many of us have observed ornately framed mission statements hanging on boardroom walls across corporate America. But sadly, for the vast majority of employees across the vast majority of these organizations, the statements have no meaningful impact on team-member pride and joy. Many struggle to see the linkage between aspirational platitudes and what they actually *do* every day. When team members can consciously connect the dots, they begin to understand the sanctity of their work.

Big Four accounting firm KPMG is an excellent example of an organization that has taken an innovative approach to ensuring cultural imperatives are properly translated across all employee job functions. Several years ago, the firm launched an organization-wide Higher Purpose initiative designed to strengthen employee pride, engagement, and emotional connection to the firm. As a pivotal component of this effort, the organization's purpose statement, "Inspire confidence. Empower change," has been infused into the hearts and minds of team members across a wide variety of channels, including print and video communications, leadership talks, social media, employee engagement activities, and live events.

Shortly after rolling out Higher Purpose, KPMG developed a user-friendly online tool that enabled teammates to creatively share how their specific work efforts were making a difference. Calling it the "10,000 Stories Challenge," the firm encouraged their twenty-seven thousand partners and employees to create digital posters (either individually or within teams) that answered the question "What do you do at KPMG?" Instructions stressed the importance of connecting the question response to the company purpose.

Bruce Pfau, former vice chair of HR and communications at KPMG, continues the story as conveyed in a 2015 *Harvard Business Review* article entitled "How an Accounting Firm Convinced Its Employees They Could Change the World":

> We offered an incentive of two extra paid days off at the end of the year if we met the 10,000 stories goal by Thanksgiving. Instead, we surpassed the goal before the Fourth of July. Soon, it became clear that the incentive was not the primary motivator—we received thousands more stories even after we announced the extra days off were assured. In a startling display of our people's pent up appetite to express the meaning of their work, by Thanksgiving we had received 42,000 stories.[10]

Reinforce What Matters

The problem with most training is that it fails to have the intended impact on the audience. Someone once said that training which doesn't lead to behavioral change is just information. In order for training to stick, it must be presented in an interesting and inspiring fashion. It should also help recipients recognize their greater purpose and reveal why the training will benefit them. But just as importantly, effective training should reinforce key concepts and principles. On more than one occasion, students in my yearlong leadership programs have asked me why I continue to review certain topics from one seminar to the next. After assuring them that I have *not* run out of content, I remind them that without ongoing repetition, they will be much less likely to retain the material or put it into actual practice, no matter how riveting my presentation skills might be!

A growing body of evidence in the field of neuroscience further supports what we intuitively already knew to be true. Repeated exposure to content over an extended period of time leads to a kind of pattern automation. For good or bad, you can literally rewire your brain. Neural pathways, comprised of neurons connected by dendrites, are created in the brain based on our habits and behaviors. As we participate in new learning activities, we are actually training our brains to form new neural pathways. The pathways get stronger with sustained repetition until the knowledge and corresponding behaviors eventually become rooted into our standard routines.

Ritz-Carlton does a masterful job of reinforcing the essential elements of their culture. For example, every employee from every property around the globe participates in a daily ten-to-fifteen-minute lineup meeting designed to enliven one of the company's venerated service standards, which consist of the Ritz-Carlton motto, three steps of service, employee credo, and service values. These standards are memorialized via laminated, wallet-sized "credo" cards and are a required accoutrement of employee uniforms / business attire. As part of each lineup, a service standard is highlighted using situational role plays, celebrating customer success stories, reviewing property-specific service breakdowns, etc. This daily cadence, fueled by senior leadership, creates a powerful shared experience where embracing organizational core values becomes second nature.

Become Master Storytellers
From the early days of human existence, the art of storytelling has played an integral role in drawing people together to pursue a shared cause. In countless instances, those most skilled at communicating their point of view win by garnering the collective commitment of their audience. Why is this the case? Brain science points to the strong correlation between storytelling and the brain chemical oxytocin. Studies indicate that oxytocin is primarily responsible for engendering empathic behavior and for motivating others to engage in cooperative activities. And what chemical releases at a rate far greater than any other does after hearing an inspiring story? You guessed it…oxytocin. No wonder we tend to more easily remember details conveyed by a good storyteller than by some talking head rambling on about a bunch of information crammed onto a PowerPoint slide!

Leaders would be well served to frequently enliven their company's purpose and core values through the use of story. Consider developing a repository of impact stories that are made possible by the amazing efforts of your workforce. I know of one organization that has produced its own electronic "video vault," which is housed in a prominent location on their company intranet site. The vault consists of a series of micro-videos highlighting the personal stories of employees who have demonstrated the company's stated purpose in some powerful way.

Every human being and every culture has a story, and new chapters are being written all the time. Look for ways to uncover, enliven, and celebrate these stories as part of an ongoing, systematic business practice.

Watch Your Words
Effective communication is essential to any organization, and this particular theme surfaces regularly as a top "opportunity for improvement" from employee engagement surveys. Furthermore, our choice of words can be a huge factor in the success of our cultural change efforts. Consider the following personal example:

In our early married years prior to having our first child, my wife (Julie) worked as a kindergarten teacher at an elementary school in Central Florida. During the course of a particular school year, Julie was asked to be a maid of honor in an out-of-town wedding for a longtime friend. In order to participate in the rehearsal practice, dinner, and other festivities, we both took a couple of vacation days off from work. Fast-forward to the following Monday morning after our trip, when several of Julie's kindergarten students rushed into the classroom to express how much they missed her. One particular little girl, though, had a very unexpected message to share.

"Mrs. Lutz, Mrs. Lutz, we missed you so much! But we sure did have fun with that *prostitute*! When can she come back to visit us?"

Several other children also chimed in. "Yeah, prostitutes are awesome!" Julie was utterly stunned until it finally dawned on her what the students were trying to communicate. Instead of "prostitute," they really meant to say "substitute." Apparently, they were big fans of the substitute teacher who had filled in the prior week.

Most of us can probably recall prior scenarios where poor word choice had a more chilling effect within our workplace. Or even worse, the complete absence of words can be the most corrosive of all. Following the initial outbreak of the COVID-19 virus and the corresponding stay-at-home orders, I spoke with a number of my business contacts across several industries. In each instance, they shared that multiple weeks had passed before they received any meaningful communications from their workplaces regarding future job security. Now granted, the uncertainties surrounding short- and long-term business impacts made it difficult for many companies to provide any definitive commentary to their workforce, but simply expressing common care and concern would have strengthened employee morale and helped ease growing angst. As a leader, what you say, or choose not to say, in the midst of crisis, speaks volumes about who you are.

Treat Everyone like a VIP

"I just wanted to give everyone a heads-up that we're expecting Michael Jordan to be in attendance this morning. That's right. I'm talking about *that* Michael Jordan. I urge you to do whatever is necessary to take care of Mr. Jordan during his visit."

You could see the fifty or so people standing in our meeting room suddenly snap to attention as soon as the director of volunteers made the announcement not too long ago at Northpoint Community Church, located in a northern suburb of Atlanta, Georgia. On any given Sunday, thousands of people attend services at Northpoint. With a church that large and respected, it is not unusual to see an occasional famous athlete, musician, or actor.

But this was at an entirely different level. We are talking about one of the most recognizable names on the face of the planet, among the greatest athletes in any sport to ever live. You could sense the energy in the room surge as the director proceeded to share a number of other less interesting announcements. Prior to releasing us to assume our various volunteer posts, the director mentioned he had one final thing to tell us.

"Oh. Just one more thing before we dismiss. Remember the part I mentioned earlier about MJ being in the building today? I was just kidding, although he *could* be here today. We have received no information that would lead us to believe that he *will* be here. Before you stuff me in a coat closet down the hall, allow me to explain myself. You see, we have been asked to provide a first-class experience for every single person we come in contact with today…rich or poor, black or white, famous or nameless, beautiful or not so beautiful, friendly or rude. Everybody is worthy of receiving our very best self. So let's commit ourselves today to fulfilling the Golden Rule—treat others the way we want to be treated."

I speak to everyone in the same way, whether he is the
garbage man or the president of the university.
—Albert Einstein

The illustration above has significant application for the organizations we represent and lead. No matter how large or geographically dispersed your company might be, your employees and your customers need to know they are more than just a number. As former US president Theodore Roosevelt so aptly pointed out decades ago, "People don't care how much you know until they know how much you care."

Be Visible

In their well-known book *In Search of Excellence*, authors Tom Peters and Robert Waterman popularized the concept of management by walking around (MBWA). As the term suggests, MBWA involves leaders taking regular time out of their workday to carefully listen to the ideas and concerns of their staff. In contrast to the more traditional approach of isolating oneself in an office, the proactive practice of MBWA, when carried out in a caring and sincere manner, has been shown to facilitate improvements in team-member trust, employee engagement, sense of purpose, innovation, and overall productivity.[11]

Former Ritz-Carlton president and COO Herve Humler was a master MBWA practitioner. Whether strolling the halls at the Ritz corporate offices or visiting one of the company's more than one hundred properties around the globe, Humler had a unique way of connecting with everyone he encountered, from senior leadership to members of the valet or housekeeping staff. Down to earth and refreshingly genuine, he recognized the importance of being "one with the people." Humler was a true gentleman actively serving other internal ladies and gentlemen with passion and humility.

Maintaining effective leader visibility may seem impractical for companies with large staff levels or multiple business locations. But the advancement of numerous technology offerings makes it easier than ever to meaningfully connect on a remote basis. More than anything, your colleagues need to feel connected to senior leadership and to a higher organizational purpose. When in-person dialogue is simply not possible, look for creative alternatives like videoconferencing (e.g., Zoom and Microsoft Teams), internal blogs, videos and podcasts, virtual "all-hands" forums, group messaging and chat tools, and digital discussion forums. Regardless of the communication mode, the key is to continuously reinforce leader commitment to the well-being and prosperity of your employees, customers, and community.

Next Steps on the Pathway-to-Purpose Journey

→ **Schedule time at your next team meeting to view Carol Dweck's highly acclaimed TED talk, "The Power of Believing You Can Improve."** Discuss the importance of living from a growth mindset. Be prepared to share a personal experience in which you found yourself slipping into a fixed mindset but were ultimately able to change your perspective for the good. Solicit ideas from the group on how the team can become more growth minded.

→ **Meet one-on-one with each of your direct reports to ensure they can *connect the dots* between their job roles and the overall corporate purpose.** Consider implementing a program similar to KPMG's "10,000 Stories Challenge" to further bolster pride and joy within your workforce. Make it a regular practice to publicly recognize the efforts of team members who exemplify your company purpose and core values.

→ **What are two to three specific steps you could take over the next thirty days to build greater trust levels among your teammates and organization?** What is your reaction to the concept of vulnerability-based trust? How would your department and/or organization rate their level of trust that senior management is acting on behalf of their best interest?

→ **How are you regularly reinforcing the cultural mores of your organization that make it uniquely differentiated?** What can you and your colleagues do to develop enhanced strategies where embracing your core values becomes embedded into the DNA of your company?

→ **How can your organization become master storytellers?** Where and how can you more effectively mine for great stories that reinforce your company purpose and core values? Consider asking some of your key customers/clients to share testimonials of how your team has served them well. Make a commitment to share a customer or employee impact as part of every team meeting.

Chapter 4

TEAMING: NURTURE COLLABORATION

The way a team plays as a whole determines its success.
You may have the greatest bunch of individual stars in the
world, but if they don't play together, the club won't
be worth a dime.
—Babe Ruth

Views of success in our formative and early adult years are largely based on *individual* achievement, with the exception of limited activities such as organized sports and the performing arts. The grades we earn in middle and high school, our performance on standardized tests, and our participation levels related to extracurricular activities largely define a pathway forward for college, trade/vocational school, or military enlistment. Likewise, our *individual* performance within each of these postsecondary venues is a pivotal factor in determining our future job prospects.

In his outstanding book *Big Potential*, author Shawn Achor says, "It is not until we enter the world of full-time job employment that our success becomes almost entirely interconnected with those we work with on a daily basis." Achor points to emerging research suggesting nearly every element of human potential, from "intelligence to creativity to leadership to personality and engagement—is interconnected with others."[1] As noted previously, we all desire to look back on our lives someday and know that we made a difference. We all want purpose and to be part of something bigger than ourselves. If this collective human yearning is legitimate, then Achor's take on interconnectedness has massive implications. You may be an organizational rock star. You may be at the very top of your chosen profession. But even at your best, you will never come close to accomplishing what an impassioned group of individuals can do together.

In today's knowledge economy, as organizations continuously increase in complexity, and the need to cooperate as a means of competitive advantage becomes a higher priority, more and more of our work is becoming team based. According to extensive study data collected by researchers Adam Grant, Reb Rebele, and Rob Cross, time spent by managers and employees in collaborative versus individual activities has risen by more than 50 percent over the past two decades.[2] The importance of cultivating our ability to work effectively within a cohesive framework cannot be overstated.

Consider Thomas Edison, one of the most prolific inventors of all time, who is credited with numerous nineteenth-century innovations like the phonograph, the incandescent light bulb, and the earliest motion picture camera. With 1,093 patents to his credit (the most of anyone in American history), Edison became one of the most famous people in the world by his mid-thirties. What historians are only now beginning to discover about Edison, however, was his masterful "ability to assemble teams and set up an organizational structure that fostered many people's creativity."[3] This fact is significant because unlike many common portrayals of Edison as a virtuoso who pumped out invention after invention in silent isolation, it appears much of Edison's brilliance lay in driving the collective genius of his contemporaries. Growing evidence suggests that the vast majority of his inventions were a collaborative effort, with Edison masterfully tapping into the ecosystem of the team around him.

In this chapter, we will explore the importance of teamwork in creating irresistible corporate cultures. As we shall see, when it comes to teamwork, one plus one definitely does not always equal two. Exceptional teamwork is always culturally accretive.

Construct the Perfect Team

In 2012, internet behemoth Google embarked upon an ambitious mission to determine why some teams perform at awe-inspiring levels, and others of seemingly comparable ilk ultimately crash and burn. A company with a history and proclivity for data-driven decision-making, Google tapped a group of their finest in-house statisticians, psychologists, sociologists, and engineers to roll out this massive initiative, affectionately known as Project Aristotle. Named after the ancient Greek philosopher's famous quote "The whole is greater than the sum of its parts," the multiyear project would unveil several groundbreaking discoveries about what does and does not make great teams tick.

From the outset, Google's experts held several working theories regarding the essential ingredients necessary to build the perfect team. For starters, human intelligence was assumed to be a critical success factor. It certainly makes sense that a group of individuals with the greater collective brain-power should easily outperform their intellectually inferior counterparts. As we shall see shortly, intelligence quotient, most often referred to as IQ, was significantly overshadowed by another form of intelligence: EQ (emotional quotient). Likewise, criteria like common interests or hobbies, similar educational or social upbringings, shared personality bents, or prior social interactions were suspected, at least in some combination, to be vital keys in the makeup of elite teamwork.

Despite an exhaustive review of more than fifty years of related academic research, and after carefully scrutinizing the traits of more than 180 teams across the Google enterprise, Abeer Dubey, a manager in the company's People Analytics Division and key leader in the Aristotle endeavor, had this to say about the group's massive research efforts: "We had lots of data, but there was nothing showing that a mix of specific personality types or skills or backgrounds made any difference. The 'who' part of the equation didn't seem to matter…At Google, we are good at finding patterns. There weren't any strong patterns here."

One pattern the research group did find similar among great teams had to do with team members having a clear grasp of *group norms*, which are the unwritten rules and often unspoken behaviors that dictate how we function when we gather. These group norms typically supersede, in predictability of success, the preferences and tendencies of the individuals that make up the team. While someone working outside the team dynamic might favor being the primary decision maker, that same individual might be willing to play more of a collaborative role within the context of group norms. Ultimately, the researchers discovered that the key norms that separated high-performing teams from dysfunctional ones had to do with how well team members treated one another.

Put differently, the presence of certain group norms inevitably increases a team's collective intelligence, whereas a group without these particular norms, even if the team members are intellectually gifted, results in mediocre or even poor overall performance. Personal brilliance alone will only get you so far.

Project Aristotle researchers found five key factors (group norms) necessary to foster exceptional teams. We will explore each of these over the following pages. The first, called psychological safety, was found to be by far the most critical, and this factor forms the foundational bedrock for the other four.[4]

Create an Environment of Well-being

Google's findings dovetail what Harvard Business School professor Amy Edmondson discovered in 1999 when she first coined the term *psychological safety*. Edmondson defines *psychological safety* as "a sense of confidence that the team will not embarrass, reject or punish someone for speaking up. It is a shared belief held by members of a team that it is safe for psychological risk-taking." In addition, Edmondson states that psychological safety "describes a team climate characterized by interpersonal trust and mutual respect in which people are comfortable being themselves."[5]

Psychological safety is one of those things that can be hard to put your finger on—sort of like falling in love or finding true inner peace. It can be quite difficult to sufficiently verbalize in pragmatic terms, but when you experience psychological safety in a very real way, you just kind of know it in your bones. Just as each of us should have the good fortune at some point in our lives to romantically connect with another in a selfless, deeply personal way, we should also have the opportunity to be on a team where our input, concerns, and contributions are truly valued.

As author Charles Duhigg described in a 2016 *New York Times* article entitled "What Google Learned from Its Quest to Build the Perfect Team": "Google's intense data collection and number-crunching have led it to the same conclusion that good managers have always known. In the best teams, members listen to one another and show sensitivity to feelings and needs."[6]

By late 2014, after nearly three years of survey collection, internal interviews, and in-depth statistical analysis, Project Aristotle researchers began sharing their findings with a cross-section of Google's fifty-one thousand team members. By doing so, the group hoped to uncover any missing research elements, particularly with regard to strategies for indoctrinating psychological safety into the overarching team dynamic. Enter Matt Sakaguchi, a mid-level manager at Google. Following a particular Project Aristotle employee presentation, Sakaguchi reached out to some of the project researchers for guidance. He shared that a group of employees he had previously managed at Google had not collaborated very well, and Sakaguchi was interested in leveraging the Aristotle results to build stronger cohesion within his new team of technical engineers.

Project Aristotle leaders provided Sakaguchi with a survey tool to help initially gauge his new team's norms. Several weeks later, Sakaguchi received the results and was disappointed to learn the group was not nearly as engaged as he had hoped. For instance, when asked to rate if the team clearly understood whether their work made a difference, members of the team provided poor to mediocre scores. Sakaguchi was particularly bothered by this because he wanted his employees to experience purpose and fulfillment in their work. He scheduled an off-site meeting with the team to discuss the survey results and how to best move forward. On a hunch that would turn out to be prophetic, Sakaguchi decided to launch the session by asking each individual to share something personal about themselves.

Sakaguchi went first. He told his team that he had stage four cancer, which had first been detected nearly thirteen years earlier in his kidney and had gradually spread to his spine. Sakaguchi had become a highly successful and respected leader at Google all while surreptitiously undergoing intensive cancer treatments. Even more disheartening, Sakaguchi shared that doctors had recently found a new spot on his liver, which appeared to be much more serious. His team, of course, was completely shocked. They had been working with Sakaguchi for ten months but had had no idea what he was going through. In recalling the episode, Sean Laurent, one of Sakaguchi's direct reports, said the following: "To have Matt stand there and tell us that he's sick and he's not going to get better and, you know, what that means. It was a really hard, really special moment."

Sakaguchi's authenticity that day had a major impact on the dynamics of the team. Individual team members began to speak more openly about things they were struggling with at work and home. They found it easier to accept one another's flaws and to encourage each other during challenging times. Sakaguchi's hunch had paid off in a major way, and it helped Project Aristotle researchers contextualize the relationship between psychological safety and emotional connection.

"I think, until the off-site, I had separated things in my head into *work* life and *life* life," Laurent said. "But the thing is, my work is my life. I spend the majority of my time working. Most of my friends I know through work. If I can't be open and honest at work, then I'm not really living, am I?" In a period of history where massive amounts of time, energy, and money are invested in the pursuit of improved personal productivity, it is easy to overlook the impacts that teamwork can have on collective productivity.[7]

It would be inaccurate to think of an environment in which psychological safety thrives as one where team members pretend to agree on everything, actively avoid all interpersonal conflict, and go out their way to ensure their colleagues' feelings are never hurt. At the end of the day, psychological safety is not about rainbows and unicorns. In many ways, this utopian construct is in direct opposition to how the psychological safety phenomenon actually works.

One of the most significant revelations any of us can have in business— or life in general—is to grasp that it is not cruel to tell people the truth in a caring and respectful manner. On the contrary, for those of us in leadership roles, I would argue that we have an ethical responsibility to provide those in our care with honest and objective feedback. Failing to engage in regular, productive conflict ultimately limits the capacity of our workforce to continuously learn and grow, which, in turn, stifles personal/collective engagement and creativity. Telling people what they need to hear is the only way to ensure they both trust you and understand you have their best interests in mind. Honest feedback is a gift when handled appropriately.

Ray Dalio is the founder of Bridgewater Associates, the world's largest hedge fund, with more than $160 billion in assets and 1,500 employees. Headquartered in Westport, Connecticut, the company has won numerous industry and workplace awards, including being named the best company to work for in the state of Connecticut by *24/7 Wall St.* In 2012, Dalio himself was named by *Time* magazine as one of the one hundred most influential people in the world.

In his best-selling book *Principles*, Dalio expounds upon the key business philosophies (or principles) that he asserts have fueled Bridgewater's renowned culture. From his standpoint, great cultures rise and fall based upon a concept he refers to as *radical transparency*. Though he does not reference the term *psychological safety* in the book or related communications, the similarities between Amy Edmondson's original research on psychological safety and Dalio's concept of radical transparency are hard to miss. In a 2017 interview with Business Insider, Dalio discusses the Bridgewater culture and his take on radical transparency:

> Let me explain what our culture is based on. I think the greatest tragedy of mankind is that people have ideas and opinions in their heads but don't have a process for properly examining these ideas to find out what's true. That creates a world of distortions. That's relevant to what we do, and I think it's relevant to all decision making. So when I say I believe in radical truth and radical transparency, all I mean is we take things that ordinarily people would hide, and we put them on the table, particularly mistakes, problems, and weaknesses. We put those on the table, and we look at them together. We don't hide them. That's what I mean by radical truth. I mean accepting reality.[8]

Furthermore, Dalio notes, "meaningful relationships are invaluable for building and sustaining a culture of excellence, because they create the trust and support that people need to push each other to do great things." These meaningful relationships lead to meaningful work, which is largely made possible through the practice of radical transparency.[9]

Psychological safety and radical transparency sound great in theory, but putting them into widespread practice across an organizational landscape can be very challenging. Most of us do not find pleasure in having our own inadequacies exposed or feeling compelled to call out the inadequacies of others. We must feel safe in order to do so. We need to know that speaking up for the greater good will not be frowned upon or held against us. At the close of this chapter, we will examine some best practices to overcome cultures fueled by collective interpersonal fear. In the meantime, here are the remaining four elements Google found to be most predictive of high-performing teams.

Dependability

I once worked with a team of ten or so colleagues in the development and rollout of a new training program at a large financial institution. This cross-functional group represented some of the best and brightest from the company's major lines of business, and we clearly had great team chemistry from the outset. Our initial weekly planning and development meetings were highly collaborative, creative, and, dare I say, even enjoyable to attend. I felt confident that our end product would be a smashing success.

But as time passed, it became increasingly clear that two of our team members were not carrying their weight, despite providing advance assurances to the group that we could count on them to do so. They repeatedly missed key milestone deliverables, thus forcing the rest of us to pick up the slack. As our official launch date approached, team stress levels spiked, fatigue kicked in, and, despite our best efforts to keep everything running smoothly, some critical action steps were not executed properly. At the end of the day, a major project rollout that could (and should) have been a real game changer was relegated to mediocrity—all because a couple of team members repeatedly failed to deliver on their commitments.

High-performing teams know they can count on their fellow colleagues to keep their promises, whereas the root cause of many underperforming ones can be traced back to individuals who talk a good game but disappear when the stakes are raised. Once the sacred bonds of trust and dependability are broken, they are not easily recovered, and the entire team dynamic suffers as a result.

Structure and Clarity

As we have discussed, teams consisting of individuals with high-level talent and intelligence are not always successful. Instead, those that work in unison toward a common purpose, speaking with one voice and a willingness to sacrifice on behalf of the greater good, most often come out on top. Everyone needs to know how they fit into the bigger picture and to understand the expected rules of engagement.

Love them or hate them, the New England Patriots professional football team has set the standard over the past couple of decades with regard to sustainable success. The organizational culture, commonly referred to as the Patriot Way, is among the most respected in the world, sports or otherwise. Winning an amazing six out of the past nineteen Super Bowls (including three of the past six) has propelled the club to elite status. As with most exceptional organizations, success for the Patriots has not been accidental. As popular author and speaker Anthony Robbins says, "Success leaves clues."

Bill Belichick, unquestionably one of the greatest coaches in NFL history, has built a sports dynasty in New England centered on a relentless commitment to preparation, personal accountability, and team over self. Belichick and his coaching staff do a remarkable job of identifying players—from bona fide superstars to undrafted rookies—who are passionate about the game and willing to sacrifice personal glory for team success. With these prerequisites in place, the staff arms them with the proper blend of structure (attention to detail, excessive repetition) and freedom (adaptability, openness to new ideas) to consistently outthink and outperform the competition. With Belichick at the helm, even a hint of selfish behavior or negative attitude could be grounds for a swift dismissal, regardless of one's status on the depth chart. Not surprisingly, and as characteristic of most high-performing teams, the physical and psychological demands embedded in the Patriots culture are not for everyone. But for those who stick around and embrace the larger picture, the rewards can be sweet indeed.[10]

Meaning

This group norm hearkens back to one of the central themes of this book: discovering that work was designed to be so much more than just labor. The untold hours we pour into our professions hold the promise of a much deeper calling and purpose. Recall the story earlier in this chapter about Matt Sakaguchi, the Google manager who courageously opened up to his team about his ongoing battle with a serious form of cancer. When asked why he didn't just quit his job in light of the health challenges, Sakaguchi revealed that helping his team learn and grow "is the most meaningful work I've ever done." He has recognized how fulfilling work can be, particularly in the context of a team. "Why would I walk away from this? Why wouldn't I spend time with people who care about me?"

Work should be personally gratifying for each of us. Discover a career that inspires you to be your best self, and you will gladly endure intermittent lows to ultimately savor the enduring highs.

> Choose a job you love and you will never have to work
> a day in your life.
> —Confucius

Recognize Your Impact

An important part of linking into our collective purpose is understanding how our work meaningfully affects organizational goals and the larger world around us. To fully grasp our impact is to draw the connection between the things we do (our behaviors) and the subsequent things we get (our results). One of our major responsibilities as leaders is to help guide our employees through this discovery process, particularly for those in job functions, such as support and administrative roles, where the connection may not always be readily apparent. The story conveyed in chapter 3, in which student workers personally observed the impacts of their solicitation efforts on behalf of future scholarship recipients, is a strong example. Let's quickly examine another relatable case study.

Few people outside the walls of San Diego–based WD-40 are likely to fully appreciate the pride and passion the company's five hundred employees (affectionately referred to as "the tribe") bring to their respective jobs each day. Granted, WD-40, the maker of the famous blue-and-yellow spray can and lubricant that stops squeaks and makes moving parts run smoothly, is not a product most of us think of when it comes to having a profound impact on humankind. It doesn't claim to cure disease or provide outstanding entertainment value or magically improve our relationship skills. But at the same time, most Americans, and untold others across the globe, are familiar with the iconic brand. Even more fascinating, millions of us have at least one can of WD-40 stashed away in our homes or workplaces right now!

With a cool $423 million in revenue in 2019 and an employee satisfaction rate of 92 percent (compared to a 32 percent rate nationwide), WD-40 is clearly hitting on all cylinders. CEO Garry Ridge and his senior leadership team do an amazing job of internalizing the company culture, which is summarized in a well-crafted purpose statement: "We exist to create positive lasting memories in everything we do. We solve problems. We make things work smoothly. We create opportunities."[11]

We will take a deeper look at key elements of the WD-40 culture later in this book, but needless to say, Ridge and his leadership are unyielding in their quest to inspire a tribe of individuals who are passionately aligned with the company's higher purpose and completely sold out to its core values. As a result, team members care deeply about their fellow colleagues and take great pride in helping customers from all walks of life solve everyday problems. According to Ridge, "Profit is the applause of doing good work and having engaged employees." By doubling down on their people and their purpose, the applause continues for WD-40, on a journey now spanning more than sixty-seven years—unconventional results and acclaim in a highly conventional industry.[12]

Purpose-driven, passionate people who are guided by
values create amazing outcomes.
—Garry Ridge

As highlighted earlier, research outcomes from Google and Project Aristotle revealed that psychological safety, to a much greater degree than the other fundamental factors of dependability, structure, meaning, and impact, is most critical to optimal-performing teams. For the remainder of this chapter, we will explore real-world ideas and practices for embracing psychological safety.

Strategies for Developing Psychological Safety

Foster Trust
At the heart of psychological safety lies the willingness of individuals to be open and honest in greater service to the goals and objectives of the team. No team will ever reach its full potential without the presence of a deep-seated belief that they can bring their true selves to work without fear of humiliation or reprisal. But what exactly is trust, and how do we make it a cornerstone tenet of our corporate culture? According to the *Oxford English Dictionary*, *trust* is "the firm belief in the reliability, truth, or ability of someone or something." Note that trust is grounded in our underlying *belief* system about something or someone.

We believe something to be true based upon our prior experiences or programming. For example, I believe the sun will rise tomorrow morning because I have witnessed it do so over and over again. By the same token, I do not believe that my neighbor's cat has the ability to speak fluent Portuguese because I have never had a meaningful conversation with a cat—or any other animal, for that matter. The point here is that our behaviors flow from our beliefs regarding what is authentic and true. The only way for a group of individuals to trust that you are sincere in wanting what's best for them is to demonstrate your trustworthiness. *In order for trust to be known, it must first be shown.*

Celebrated author and University of Houston professor Brene Brown has spent the last two decades studying the emotional dynamics of courage and vulnerability. Brown's 2010 TEDxHouston talk, "The Power of Vulnerability," is one of the top five most viewed TED talks ever. In her work, Brown points out that most of us were raised to believe that vulnerability is a sign of weakness. Letting our guard down and revealing potential inadequacies or fears is generally frowned upon, particularly in Western society. Brown's research, however, has turned this theory on its head.[13]

It turns out that vulnerability is not a sign of weakness after all. It is actually an indicator of strength, allowing us to purposefully and boldly wade into difficult situations. Vulnerability is a vital component of a successful team because it enables the building of trust among team members. Though vulnerability certainly does not have to entail sharing your deepest secrets with your teammates, it should absolutely include consciously revealing your human side (admitting when you don't know the answer, taking responsibility for a failure, providing difficult but constructive feedback to a peer or subordinate, choosing not to react aggressively when someone criticizes your work or point of view, etc.).

As leaders, it is incumbent on us to set a tone of safety and security, where our team members feel comfortable bringing their full repertoire of talents and ingenuity to bear. Encouraging circles of safety in the workplace positions us as an employer of choice and provides our businesses with a distinct competitive advantage in the marketplace. It is in this type of environment where collective genius and employee engagement are most likely to thrive. Says Brown, "Vulnerability is the birthplace of creativity, innovation and change."

Beware of Cultural Saboteurs
A single individual, no matter how well intentioned, cannot construct an irresistible culture in isolation. They can certainly conceive a desired future and begin orchestrating a game plan to put it into motion, but the only way to bring the culture to life is through a dedicated tribe of capable and purpose-driven individuals. Beware, however, that one or two ill-intentioned people can absolutely destroy a culture.

In chapter 2, we explored the concept of "burning the boats," where leaders identify cultural non negotiables that may not be compromised regardless of the situation, things that leadership is willing to "die for," like honesty, integrity, and mutual respect. I would submit that the presence of what I call "cultural saboteurs" should be viewed as a burn-the-boats issue within your organization. By allowing certain individuals to subvert your company culture, irrespective of their production levels or your personal desire to not deal with the proverbial elephant in the room, you are essentially communicating to the larger workforce that your core values are negotiable and situational. It would be similar to parents constantly extolling the importance of integrity to their kids only to look the other way upon learning their child was accepted into a top-flight university primarily because they cheated on an entrance exam. For the offending child, the interpretation will likely be that "the rules are negotiable as long as I continue performing." For the remaining children, skepticism and doubt are likely to take root. "I only have to follow the rules in certain situations. Integrity must not be such a big deal to my parents after all."

How much are you willing to tolerate when it comes to a lack of adherence to your company values? Burning the boats for the greater good of the organization can often be uncomfortable and even frightening, but leadership requires the courage to stand in the gap and do the right thing. And sometimes the right thing entails extracting toxic employees from the boat before the entire culture goes down in flames.

Seek to Understand Why
In his famous book *The Seven Habits of Highly Effective People*, author Stephen Covey tells the story of his experience one Sunday morning on a New York subway. Covey recalls the subway being particularly quiet and relaxing that day. Some passengers focused intently on their book or newspaper, others gazed around seemingly lost in thought, and still others rested silently with their eyes closed. At a particular stop, a man and his young children jumped on the subway car. The kids immediately turned what had been a peaceful scene into a three-ring circus, becoming increasingly loud and rambunctious as the minutes passed. The scene continued to unfold as the

children began throwing things and even grabbing people's belongings. And all along, the man appeared totally oblivious and apathetic to the situation.

Finally, with what he deemed to be particular patience and constraint, Covey turned to the man and said, "Sir, your children are really disturbing a lot of people. I wonder if you couldn't control them a little more?" The gentleman looked up from his apparent stupor, as if realizing for the first time what had been unfolding in front of him. In a highly troubled tone, he said, "Oh, you're right. I guess I should do something about it. We just came from the hospital, where their mother died about an hour ago. I don't know what to think, and I guess they don't know how to handle it either."[14]

Sometimes things can be very different than they seem. There are some on your team who will not initially feel comfortable with the idea of speaking up or risk-taking. Perhaps your reluctant new hire shared her point of view with a prior manager and was shamed for doing so. Or maybe another employee you brought over from another division opened up once about a job failure and was publicly chastised for being "totally incompetent." Great leadership often entails "peeling back the onion" to understand what drives your people to behave in certain ways.

Do not underestimate the importance of getting to know your teammates and connecting with them on an emotional level. Encourage them to go outside their comfort zones, and reassure them that regardless of prior experiences, they are in a safe environment where their opinions and input matter. And most importantly, model the way for your team. Share with them your personal *why*, and have the courage to reveal your human, interpersonal side. Ask how you can support them in achieving their dreams.

Avoid Groupthink

One telltale sign that psychological safety has not taken hold in your organization is the absence of any meaningful conflict. A lack of tension or discord may be an indicator of a phenomenon known as *groupthink*, where team members consciously avoid upsetting the balance of the group. More simply, individuals in an environment infected with groupthink seek to avoid "rocking the boat" at any cost.

A dynamic where everyone merely pretends to be on the same page, while withholding true candor, is one sure to be void of employee passion and purpose. It is also a culture where continuous improvement and innovation are wholly stifled and where organizations ultimately go to die. The power of collective genius is essentially rendered meaningless in the presence of groupthink.

According to author Ray Dalio, "The fact that no one seems concerned doesn't mean nothing is wrong." Dalio goes on to say that groupthink can ultimately lead to "a spiral of silence" where an individual's perception of the majority opinion suppresses their willingness to share challenging questions.

True psychological safety is largely characterized by a healthy dose of debate and fervent back and forth. It is not just that everyone's voice matters. It actually runs much deeper than that. Everyone's voice absolutely matters, but providing one's unvarnished point of view is essential to team breakthroughs. To get optimal performance from your team requires a commitment to speaking truth, even when it is awkward and potentially messy.

To combat groupthink in team settings, first give team members the opportunity to provide their opinions independently, without the influence of the group. For instance, when conducting brainstorming exercises, I establish ground rules whereby the first round of ideas is all about quantity, not quality. No "idea blocking" is allowed in round one.

Similarly, when asking for advice or input, I typically withhold my personal thoughts upfront and ask team members to provide their opinions in separate emails. Probably the most important way to avert groupthink, though, is to establish group norms in which conflict and differences of opinion are not only encouraged but also communicated to be a necessary element of effective team collaboration.

Promote Principled Failure
Karen Adolph is professor of psychology and neural science at New York University. As part of her research, Adolph studies the acquisition of motor skills in toddlers and corresponding impacts on their learning and development over time. In a 2012 study focused on a group of twelve-to-nineteen-month-old babies attempting to walk, Adolph and her colleagues found that

the toddlers fell an average of seventeen times per hour. *Seventeen* times per hour! That's practically a fall every three minutes…over and over and over again! The degree of resilience observed in mere babes is remarkable, and it speaks volumes to our older selves about how easily we cave at the slightest amount of challenge or resistance. How many of us in our current adult states are willing to get knocked down at *anything* more than a time or two and keep trying? How about seventeen times per hour? It is inconceivable.[15]

Failure is just a necessary part of the process on the path to success. Early in life, we are encouraged by the world to think outside the box, to "rub some dirt on it" and get back in the game, to believe anything is possible if we just don't give up. But as we reach adolescence and beyond, the message becomes markedly different. We are told to stay in our lanes, to not rock the boat, and to accept the hand dealt to us. If at first you do not succeed, then just accept your inadequacy, throw in the towel, and revert back to what comes easy. Or even better, look for someone else or something else to blame.

As we develop, society informs us that certain activities are to be avoided at all costs, particularly if they involve even the remote possibility of failing. We are conditioned to believe (both directly and indirectly) that failing is proof positive of our human inadequacy and lack of self-worth. At some point along the journey of life, falling down is no longer an acceptable outcome of well-intentioned effort but rather an unvarnished representation of who we are. It can become a literal state of being.

In our role as corporate influencers and change agents, we have the opportunity to shift the mindsets of our teams around the notion of what I call *principled failure*. Principled failure is any failure that occurs in pursuit of a noble cause, as opposed to one fueled by unethical behavior or in opposition to an established core value. Failing to land the new corporate account despite your team's best (and honest) effort would be a principled failure, whereas lying about the performance capabilities of your product or service in an attempt to close the deal would be an unacceptable failure.

Calling back to our earlier discussion regarding vulnerability, sharing our own stories of failure and ultimate redemption helps build assurance within our teams that falling down is a necessary part of continuous growth and development. Additionally, Stanford University professor Carol Dweck emphasized the importance of praising individual and collective *effort*, regardless of the outcome. "When people believe their performance is an indication of their ability or intelligence, they are less likely to take risks—for fear of a result that would disconfirm their ability. But when people believe that performance reflects effort and good strategy, they are eager to try new things and willing to persevere despite adversity and failure." It is only through our failures that we experience success.

> There is no easier way to invite experimentation and learning than to share stories about your own mistakes. As a leader, your acknowledgement of your personal mistakes will give others permission to experience failure and go on to learn and recover with dignity and increased capability.
> —Liz Wiseman

Closing Thoughts

One final thing related to psychological safety before we wrap up this chapter. As I write, we are in the midst of some extremely challenging times in the United States and around the world. The COVID-19 pandemic changed the rules of the game for millions of leaders and employees who were challenged to operate in a largely remote environment. The "new normal" is likewise uncertain, as face-to-face collaboration will be cumbersome for some time to come. As Simon Sinek says in his best-selling book *Leaders Eat Last*, "It's not how smart the people in the organization are; it's how well they work together that is the true indicator of future success or the ability to manage through struggle."[16] We are indeed knee-deep in uncharted waters, thus presenting an optimal time in history for leaders to step into the forefront and foster a safe haven for employees to feel heard and valued.

Wrapped around the uncertainties of the pandemic are the topics of diversity, inclusion, and justice. People of all races and creeds have a God-given right to experience psychological safety in the context of life and work.

Progress in overcoming issues of the heart will not happen in a vacuum. They will require honest and unimpeded dialogue among employees across all organizational levels, but as with all critical endeavors, it is most effective when sanctioned and embraced from senior leadership. We have a massive opportunity to take the lead in driving positive change for those who feel their voices have been stifled for far too long. Perhaps our dedication to directing enduring change in our workplaces will provide a springboard for progress in other arenas as well.

> Unless you are running a one-person company, where everything begins and ends with you, then everything begins and ends with your team.

Next Steps on the Pathway-to-Purpose Journey

→ **Have your senior leadership team read Charles Duhigg's 2016 *New York Times* article "What Google Learned from Its Quest to Build the Perfect Team."** Ask them to be prepared to discuss their insights at the next leader meeting. Solicit team feedback regarding perceptions of how widely psychological safety is embraced within the organization.

→ **Conduct an informal survey with your direct team to gauge current levels of psychological safety.** Consider using the following statements (five-point scale, from "strongly agree" to "strongly disagree"), crafted by expert Amy Edmondson, professor of leadership and management at Harvard Business School:

1. If you make a mistake on this team, it is often held against you.
2. Members of this team are able to bring up problems and tough issues.
3. People on this team sometimes reject others for being different.
4. It is safe to take a risk on this team.
5. It is difficult to ask other members of this team for help.
6. No one on this team would deliberately act in a way that undermines my efforts.
7. Working with members of this team allows me to utilize my unique skills and talents.

→ **To what extent do you feel groupthink is a problem within your organization?** How about within your specific team? What steps will you take to ensure authenticity and innovation are not being stifled as a result of others trying to avoid conflict?

→ **Are there individuals within your company who are widely recognized as cultural saboteurs?** Work with human resources and applicable divisional leadership to formulate a time-based plan to either recover the designated team members or exit them from the organization.

Chapter 5

COACHING: UNLEASH POTENTIAL

I t is clear that the senior leadership of most organizations genuinely wants to cultivate workplaces in which employees feel valued for their unique contributions, where they are inspired to continuously learn and grow, and where they can freely collaborate within a community of passionate colleagues. As we have discovered, however, these types of environments do not happen without a well-coordinated strategy in which executive purpose and mission are in lockstep with the unique capabilities of the overall workforce.

Despite its best efforts, an executive team cannot by itself successfully cascade and operationalize irresistible cultures. It is this critical reality that magnifies what is perhaps the most common demise of culture transformation efforts: poorly defining and underutilizing the optimal role of managers. Though the cultural heartbeat of an organization always emanates from the C-suite, those charged with the daily oversight of others ultimately bring the heartbeat to life. Managers are the cultural and operational bridge between leadership's vision and the hard realities of the front line. Collectively, they serve as the primary means to either enliven the organizational mission or irreparably destroy it.

Think about it for a moment. Managers have extreme influence over their employees. Outside of a spouse or significant other, a boss arguably wields the most power to make the life of another human being either magical or miserable. Examine the backstory of nearly every successful business leader, and you will discover one or more amazing managers who pushed, prodded, and encouraged them along the way to maximize their potential.

On the opposite end of the spectrum are dreadful managers who leave a deadly trail of emotional and psychological carnage in their wake. Unfortunately, more of us than not have been adversely affected, even permanently scarred, by these types of individuals. The well-worn axiom rings true: "Employees don't leave companies. They leave managers."

Just for kicks, I did a quick internet search using the keywords "bad boss stories." More than 315 million results instantly surfaced! Of course, some stories were of the extremely disturbing variety, involving physical and/or sexual harassment, as well as a host of blatant discriminatory practices. Others, while less lurid, were equally bizarre and inexcusable. I will share a sampling of some of the less graphic accounts on the following pages, beginning with this one:

Toxic Boss Example 1

When I resigned, my boss asked for more than the normal two-week period. He wanted as much time as possible to find a replacement. Since my new job didn't start for six weeks, I found it easy to comply with his wishes. After three weeks I told my Boss I could no longer work weekends because I was moving out-of-state. However, sure enough, despite my requested restrictions, I was scheduled to work all seven days in my final week of work. "I can't work Saturday and Sunday," I told my Boss. "You've had the last two weekends off," he replied. "You have to work or I will fire you." "I've already quit," I told him. "I am working this week as a favor to you." "You're FIRED!" he shrieked. "Fine." I shrugged and started out the door. Before I could reach the door my Boss caught me. He said, "What are you doing? You can't leave yet! You're not fired until the end of your shift!!"[1]

Some might argue that the example above—and so many others like it—is the exception to the rule, that only the most bizarre and most heinous cases are reported and highlighted for mass consumption. Though this contention may have some validity, growing research suggests a huge opportunity exists to reevaluate the appropriate role of managers in the workplace.

For example, 80 percent of workers that participated in a recent study would rather have a new boss than a 20 percent pay raise.[2] How alarming is that?

Or consider a Monster.com survey which found that 76 percent of workers looking to leave their current employer blamed the presence of a "toxic" boss for their unhappiness.[3] Would you be shocked to hear that three of four employees say their boss is the worst and most stressful part of their job?[4] Perhaps not; particularly if you are personally struggling with a superior who is making your life miserable.

Of course, the impact of toxic managers places a heavy burden on employers from a financial standpoint. American companies alone spend an estimated $360 billion in healthcare costs combatting the effects of bad bosses.[5]

> **Toxic Boss Example 2**
> I had a job working at a summer camp during college. I had worked at this camp for five summers. This particular summer my best friend unexpectedly died from heart failure and I took leave to go to the funeral. When I returned, my grandfather was on his deathbed and my mother asked me to request more time off. Obviously upset, I approached my Boss and explained the situation. She said "Well, you're just going to have to get over it and get on with your life. I can't let you go again." My grandfather died the next week. When I told my Boss, she said, "You should have planned better, you have no bereavement time left."[6]
>
> We have clearly seen, both factually and anecdotally, the power of a manager to control the cultural narrative for her team. The quality of the employee experience is in direct proportion to the effectiveness of a boss in helping team members feel comfortable bringing their whole hearts to the workplace. Fair or not, team member perceptions of their workplace environment, and the levels of engagement employees ultimately feel within a company, are disproportionately derived from how they experience their direct manager.

Redefine the Role of Bosses

In the 2019 *Wall Street Journal* number one best seller *It's the Manager*, authors Jim Clifton (chairman/CEO of Gallup) and Jim Harter (chief scientist, Workplace, Gallup) contend that while the world's workplace has undergone massive change over the course of history, the practice of *management* has been stuck in time for decades. In the book, Clifton and Harter unpack key Gallup workplace findings drawn from years of research and data tracking, including millions of in-depth interviews of employees and managers across 160 countries. Of the top fifty-two most critical findings unearthed by Gallup, one stands above all others in terms of overall significance. Listen to Clifton and Harter explain in their own words:

> Most CEOs and CHROs are probably thinking…"What can I do right now to get better outcomes? What lever do I pull to make wholesale changes in my culture so it aligns with the new will and future of work?"
>
> Of all the codes Gallup has been asked to crack dating back 80 years to our founder, George Gallup, the single most profound, distinct and clarifying finding—***ever***—is probably this one: **70 percent of the variation in team engagement is determined solely by the *manager*.**[7] (bold and italics added)

Did you catch that? Gallup claims that the single most important driver in team-member engagement is the quality and effectiveness of company managers. They are the conduit between the vision from the top and the hard realities on the front line. Ideally, managers are your most devoted employees and your most constructive critics. According to Gallup, senior leaders should allocate at least 70 percent of their time, effort, and investment on their manager population—ensuring they have the right ones in the right spots, equipping them with the resources necessary to become exceptional leaders, holding them accountable to a set of clear performance metrics, and properly rewarding them for their hard work and growth mindset.

So, now that we know the long-term path to cultural excellence resides in the hands of our managers, where should we begin? What steps should we take to make certain our managers can competently stand in the gap and become the cultural champions we need them to be? We must first shift our traditional perspective of managers as *bosses* to a new paradigm of managers as *coaches*. Whereas a *boss* is commonly defined as one who exercises authority over others, a *coach* is one who inspires others to go where they would not normally go so they can achieve what they would not otherwise achieve, all while *still* ensuring the financial prosperity of the business.

A conventional boss sees subordinates as they currently are, while a coach sees others as they could someday become. Likewise, a boss generally operates from a reactive posture, leveraging old-school command-and-control tactics to drive desired performance outcomes. A great coach takes a proactive stance with employees, seeking to continuously shed light on how their efforts fuel the larger organizational purpose. Which would you rather work for, a boss or a coach? Reference figure 5.1 below for additional key philosophical and operational differences.

Dr. Atul Gawande is a distinguished endocrine and general surgeon at Brigham and Women's Hospital, a professor at the Harvard School of Public Health, and the writer of four *New York Times* best-selling books. In a 2018 TED talk, entitled "Everybody Needs a Coach," Gawande told the story of his career journey as a young, inexperienced doctor to ultimately becoming one of the most accomplished surgeons in his field. As Gawande pointed out in his talk, for the first several years of his practice, he experienced marked improvements in patient outcomes, as validated by a steady drop in surgical complication rates.

After five years or so, Gawande noticed his performance had plateaued and he was no longer improving. Never one to rest on his laurels, Gawande made the decision to do something highly unusual in the medical profession, particularly at his advanced skill level. He hired a coach, in this case a retired medical colleague, to observe him in his operating room during surgical procedures. Gawande recalled his certainty that his performance during the first observed procedure went flawlessly, only to find out during the debrief that his new coach had written a full page of notes for his consideration.

"Just small things," his coach explained. "Did you notice that the light had swung out of the wound during the case? You spent about half an hour just operating off the light from reflected surfaces." "Another thing I noticed," he said, "is your elbow goes up in the air every once in a while. That means you are not in full control. A surgeon's elbows should be down at their sides resting comfortably. So that means if you feel your elbow going in the air, you should get a different instrument, or just move your feet."

According to Gawande, the experience brought a completely new level of awareness. The coach essentially served as Gawande's copilot, seeing and hearing things the surgeon was not picking up on himself. Though the feedback provided that day and following subsequent procedures was at times difficult to hear, Gawande learned to embrace it as an opportunity to further stretch himself in pursuit of mastery. Within two months of the initial coaching, Gawande found himself improving once again, and after a full year his complications dropped to an all-time low.[8]

Toxic Boss Example 3

On Monday, my Boss approached me at 4:00 PM with an emergency assignment. He had an important meeting early the following morning and needed a new version of a 400-page document. I worked the all-nighter, made the updates, and left the manual on his desk. I left to go home at 7AM the next morning. When I came to work that Wednesday, I asked his secretary about the important, emergency, client meeting. She said, "Oh, he decided to cancel. He took a few vacation days instead."[9]

Topic	Bosses	Coaches
Definition	Are in authority over employees Make decisions or exercise authority	Unleash the potential of others as a means of optimizing their performance Motivate others to go where they would not normally go so they can achieve what they would not otherwise achieve
Mindset	Operate from a have-to mindset	Operate from a want-to mindset
Leadership Style	Command and control	Collaborate and influence
Focus	Focus first on fixing team-member behaviors (task based) Only focus on results	Focus first on addressing team-member beliefs (people based) Focus on effort as well as results
Employee Orientation	Concentrate on past mistakes Are transaction based	Concentrate on future possibilities Are relationship based
People versus Process	Primarily *manage* processes	Primarily *lead* people
Meetings	Conduct team meetings only when there is a perceived need (reactive) Meet 1:1 with direct reports when there is a problem or performance issue	Huddle up on a regular basis (proactive) Meet 1:1 with direct reports on a regularly scheduled basis (recommended weekly)

FIGURE 5.1

Suppose we were to randomly sample a group of world-class corporate professionals. One commonality we would be sure to find, whether serving in a formal or informal capacity, is the existence of a committed coach, someone who helped their "student" drill down deeply into their potential in order to achieve extraordinary feats. Over the next several pages, we will investigate the key coaching strategies employed by effective managers everywhere.

Key Roles of a Coach

Help Them See What They Cannot See on Their Own

As the great philosopher Socrates once said, "To know thyself is the beginning of wisdom." Knowing thyself, practically speaking, is significantly easier said than done. It brings to mind an old maxim, which says, "It's hard to see the picture when you're inside the frame." Indeed, sometimes we need someone we respect and trust to point out our blind spots.

In the early years of my career, I took a popular personality assessment as part of an in-house leadership development program. I remember reviewing the post assessment report, which highlighted my strengths and areas for improvement. Everything seemed to be spot on, with the exception of my uncertainty with regard to one particular section. The report noted that I should be wary of potentially coming across to others as snarky. Snarky? I wasn't exactly sure what snarky meant, but it sure didn't sound good to me. After doing a little research, I discovered that the term refers to someone who is crotchety or snappish. Huh? In layman's terms, it translates to ill-tempered, curt, or flat-out rude. At this point, I reassured myself that no personality test is 100 percent accurate, and I vowed to confirm the obvious inaccuracy during dinner that evening with my wife.

Just as planned, I explained my dilemma to Julie at the dinner table. "Hey, honey. I got the results back today from a personality assessment I took recently at work. The report was consistent with what I know to be true about myself except for one major thing. It said some people might view me as snarky, meaning cranky or rude. Isn't that weird?" Dead silence. "Um, why are you looking at me like that and being so quiet?" I could see a small smirk come over her face as she responded incredulously, "Jamey, I hate to crash your party, but you might want to take that feedback to heart!"

Effective coaches, like my wife in this particular story, speak truth to our blind spots. They also have a way of bringing instant credibility to a potentially difficult conversation.

Challenge Them to Stretch Themselves

Nearly thirty years ago, a group of scientists launched a very unconventional project named Biosphere 2. The project consisted of a 3.14-acre biodome (a type of greenhouse), complete with numerous miniature ecosystems, including a rain forest, desert, ocean, mangrove swamp, savanna, and farm. The biodome was completely self-contained, meaning no air, water, soil, or other elements could enter or exit. Among the major goals of Biosphere 2 was to harvest new insights into the interrelationships between various organisms and their environments, and to fashion an initial framework for potential biodomes in space and beyond.

One of the early observations that initially baffled the Biosphere 2 community had to do with the strange behavior of the tree population. Researchers noted that trees matured much more quickly in the biodome than in the outside world, and after reaching a certain height, they would literally collapse to the ground under their own weight! Upon further investigation, it was determined that the absence of wind inside was the underlying cause.

In the natural world, constant and often imperceptible levels of wind create constant stress on trees and plants. Because the biodome was so tightly contained, there was essentially no moving air inside. The trees therefore did not experience the typical resistance and stress found in outdoor environments. Without such stressors, the trees were unable to produce reaction bark, ultimately causing them to buckle in what would otherwise appear to be the safest and most sheltered environment possible.[10]

The presence of wind makes a tree stronger and allows it to mature without being compromised. Employees need stress to help them build a solid foundation as well. Be careful not to exert too much pressure/stress, or it could uproot the tree, like a tornado or hurricane. In our role as leaders and coaches, it is incumbent upon us to challenge employees to venture outside their comfort zone. Standing pat, or merely maintaining the status quo, throttles growth, as we learned earlier in the case of Dr. Awul Gawande. Learning is *supposed* to feel uncomfortable.

Good timber does not grow with ease: the stronger the
wind, the stronger the trees.
—J. Willard Marriott

Whereas we should constantly identify opportunities to move our people beyond their normal comfort levels, it is also critical that we remain thoughtful in our approach. Consider, for example, a particular person's aversion to public speaking, which, according to the National Institute of Mental Health, affects 73 percent of the population and ranks as the fourth-most-common human phobia behind death, spiders, and heights.[11] It would be cruel and irresponsible for a manager to demand that their employee simply "armor up" prior to delivering a formal sales presentation to a room full of potential clients. No matter how well intentioned, this approach to coaching would likely catapult an inexperienced speaker straight into panic zone. Clearly, a more reasonable approach would be for the manager and employee to collaborate in identifying a series of realistic milestones to eventually culminate in the aforementioned sales presentation:

1. Employee repeatedly delivers presentation alone in front of mirror.

2. Employee presents one-on-one with manager, who provides initial round of constructive feedback.

3. Manager videotapes subsequent presentation round and provides additional feedback.

4. Employee delivers presentation to a small group of trusted teammates and makes final enhancements based upon input.

5. Employee delivers formal presentation.

6. Manager provides post-presentation feedback to be incorporated into framework for future speaking opportunities.

The goal here is to systematically staircase individuals into the *learning zone*, thus stretching them to a point of healthy challenge without pushing them into the zone of panic.

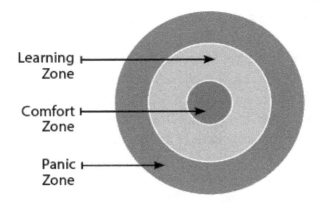

FIGURE 5.2

Foster Belief through Encouragement and Inspiration
One of the most significant gifts a coach can offer an employee is an unwavering belief in their potential to grow and overcome adversity. On occasion, it will be necessary for employees to actually *borrow* their manager's belief in them, until such time that they develop a sufficient level of confidence in themselves. A critical way to generate self-belief within the ranks of your team is through a healthy dose of encouragement and inspiration. Imagine an athletic team that is woefully underperforming and in the midst of an extended losing streak. A series of injuries, ill-timed miscues, and bad breaks has the players doubting their ability to pull themselves out of a deepening hole of uncertainty and despair. Now more than ever, the team is in dire need of human resuscitation.

It is at this point that great coaches inevitably rise to the occasion, bringing belief and hope to a season of life teetering on the brink of disaster. These individuals lock onto a preferred future and do not allow past failures to paralyze them. Note that I am certainly not saying we should ignore insights from the past as part of the continuous improvement process. My point is that leaders must take the learnings, incorporate them into a future game plan, and expeditiously move on, not allowing themselves, or their teammates, to be swallowed up by fear and uncertainty.

The most successful coaches in sports, business, and life constantly inspire and relentlessly encourage. They fight the urge to hang their heads when things go poorly, knowing that they are the models of hope within their sphere of influence. Great coaches understand that getting desired results is more than just *X*s and *O*s. As important as talent and preparation are, they will only get us so far on the journey to success. The mental and emotional aspects of the game ultimately trump everything else. In times of real challenge, the true value of a coach lies in creating a shared belief in future possibilities instead of past realities.

Pave the Way Forward (and, If Necessary, Get Out of the Way)
In his book *Unlocking Potential*, Michael Simpson provides important insights into the role of a coach to properly position employees for ongoing growth and development: "As an executive coach, I have found it helpful to ask employees and leaders all over the world this key talent question: 'How many of you possess far more talent, drive, capability, passion, and experience than your current job requires or even allows you to express?' Overwhelmingly, people raise their hands in quiet desperation and say they are undervalued, underutilized, or both."[12]

I don't know about you, but Simpson's question makes the hair rise up on my arms. There are few things more demoralizing than to feel marginalized and powerless. While employees certainly have an obligation to own their long-term career paths, the responsibility of managers to help pave the way forward should not be discounted.

What does paving the way look like in practical terms? More times than not, it boils down to a process of intentional team-member discovery. It is about taking the time to get to know your people, understanding what drives them, and creating an environment where they can blossom. For instance, let's say you learn that Cassandra, your talented human resources coordinator, has a flair for creative design. With this in mind, you use your influence to ensure she receives an invitation to join a cross-department project team charged with overhauling the company intranet site. Or perhaps you discover through your regular one-on-one meetings with Nathan that he has a heart for kids growing up in disadvantaged homes. By tapping into your extensive business network, you learn of an available board seat for a local nonprofit focused on the challenges of inner-city youth. Several phone calls later, and you have set the stage for Nathan to lean into an opportunity that would have otherwise not been available to him.

Managers commonly grapple with developing their teams for another critical reason: they overshadow their employees. Perhaps it is the result of an unintended carryover from our roles as parents, in which we tend to go out of our way to shelter our kids from failure, pain, and uncertainty. Or maybe we struggle to empower our workforce because it is really difficult to relinquish personal control. Regardless of the underlying rationale, we must be careful to monitor our personal motivations so as not to stifle employee progress.

Consider the banyan fig, a fascinating tree descended from the mulberry family and native to the Indian subcontinent. The banyan regularly reaches up to one hundred feet tall, with a massive canopy that can spread across several acres. The largest known banyan tree alive today is located in the Indian state of Andhra Pradesh and can shelter up to twenty thousand people![13] The extreme density of the banyan provides shade and protection from the elements, but at the same time, it completely chokes out the sun, effectively eliminating any possibility for ground cover or plant life. Many leaders are like banyan trees. They protect their people, but nothing grows under them. By constantly protecting our team members, we suppress their development and lead them to believe we lack faith in their ability to contribute in a meaningful way.

Reimagine Accountability

We will spend some highly focused time in the following chapter exploring the nature and importance of accountability in the workplace, but for now, I will preview a few initial thoughts for your consideration:

- Western society generally views the concept of *accountability* in a highly negative light. When people learn they are being held responsible for a particular outcome, the tendency is to perceive accountability as an unwanted form of punishment on the heels of failure. Managers serving as coaches, however, see this dynamic much differently. Instead of weaponizing the threat of accountability as an employee fear tactic, they position it as a developmental tool to foster continuous job growth. In my career, I have found that most employees genuinely want to know where they stand in their job roles. They want to know where they stack up in comparison to a predefined set of standards, and while they may not think of this desire as a call for accountability, that is exactly what it is!

- One of the most destructive things we can do as coaches is to establish standards of accountability and fail to provide direction or clarity on how to achieve them. This is the epitome of setting your team members up to fail. Left on a deserted island to fend for themselves, even your most capable employees will likely become disenchanted and increasingly susceptible to defection.

- Hold your people accountable out of love. It is not okay to sugarcoat the truth because you are concerned about hurting someone's feelings. Coaches are reality whisperers. Telling it like it is, when properly sprinkled with empathy and compassion, is in the best interest of your employee, your team, and the overall enterprise.

Provide a Constant Flow of Feedback

Can you imagine a successful sports coach (at any level) who provided their players with individualized feedback just once or twice a season? It would not happen, at least not if the coach had serious aspirations of being around very long. Constant feedback is the lifeblood of player development in the athletic world. Without it, players lack a reliable and objective pathway to improvement, which will severely compromise their growth and the overall direction and morale of the team. No rational coach on the court or gridiron withholds constructive feedback, yet it happens all the time in the business arena. According to Gallup research, employees who receive daily feedback from their manager are *three times* more likely to be engaged than those who receive feedback once a year or less.[14]

So clearly, regular communication is essential, but is just any old coaching feedback going to bring out the best in our teammates? Additional reporting by Gallup suggests the answer is unequivocally *no*! Only 23 percent of surveyed respondents think their managers provide them with meaningful feedback.[15] Stated differently, more than three of four employees are skating by without feedback that helps them meaningfully grow or that recognizes them for a job well done. Effective coaching feedback consists of the proper balance of praise/recognition and thoughtful conversation regarding growth and improvement opportunities. In addition, feedback sessions should extend beyond basic transactional dialogue around success metrics and business outcomes. Employees thrive when their coaches connect with them as human beings as well, leading to greater levels of trust and motivation.

I am often asked about the ideal cadence for conducting feedback sessions. I view this from a couple of different perspectives. First, feedback on the whole should be continuous. Going back to our sports analogy, the best coaches observe, acknowledge, and direct their players as a standard element of each practice, game, and film review. What's more, these coaching interactions always take place as close to real time as possible. If the offensive lineman keeps missing his blocking assignment, the coach should address it in the moment, not two days later as an afterthought. Now is better than later, and now makes later better.

The same recommendation holds true when it comes to coaching in the corporate world. In my prior consulting work, I have regularly seen leaders get this principle all wrong. By the time a behavioral concern is finally communicated by the manager, particulars of the situation have largely faded, other issues have leapfrogged in priority, and an important teaching moment has been compromised. Commit to a culture of continuous, informal feedback (both positive and negative) that is delivered in a timely and straightforward fashion. What you fail to deal with right away will likely deal with you later!

In addition to the largely spontaneous, reactive brand of feedback coaching just outlined, you will also want to develop a separate, more structured meeting cadence with your team. I recommend scheduling weekly thirty-to-forty-five-minute meetings with each of your direct reports. Here are some basic guidelines to follow:

- Encourage your team members to take personal ownership of weekly one-on-ones. Remind them that the meetings are being held for their benefit and as a tool to help them become a better version of themselves.

- Communicate that your primary roles in this one-on-one process are twofold: (1) to help clear the path for any obstacles that may be hindering their progress toward individual or team-based goals and objectives; and (2) to provide coaching feedback on developmental opportunities, recognize individual/collective wins, and touch on team-member progress in pursuit of future career aspirations and growth.

- Begin each meeting by requesting a status update of agreed-upon deliverables and action steps from the prior session.

- Regularly encourage your direct reports to reach out between meetings regarding any challenges or support needs.

- Seek regular input from your employees on ways to improve departmental morale, productivity, and innovation.

Recognize When Coaching Won't Help

Richard was a highly seasoned and tenured salesperson who led his company in sales every year. He was the ultimate revenue-generating rainmaker and could be counted on to reach (and exceed) his numbers even during challenging economic downturns. Richard's networking skills were second to none, and his clients loved him because of his responsiveness and ability to make deals happen. His product knowledge, reputation in the market, and positive impact on company profitability would appear to have made him the consummate employee.

But despite all of Richard's finer points, he had one Achilles' heel that would ultimately prove to be his downfall. You see, nearly all of Richard's colleagues disliked him. They viewed him as one of the most self-absorbed, cynical, backbiting, and condescending human beings they had ever been around. Richard was very aware of the disharmony he was fostering within the enterprise. His direct manager and multiple members of the senior leadership team, including the chief human resources officer, worked very hard to mold Richard into a kinder, gentler version of himself but to no avail.

The situation finally reached a boiling point, and the organization was faced with either continuing to tolerate Richard's destructive behavior or bidding him farewell in spite of his otherworldly production levels. In the end, the CEO chose the latter, effectively reinforcing to everyone that a culture grounded on the principles of care, cooperation, and collaboration is superior to the bottom-line contributions of a single sales mercenary. Beware of culture killers, and make sure you and your senior leaders get really clear on the types of behaviors that will not be tolerated within your organization. Despite your best coaching efforts, there will be some who either cannot or will not conform to cultural standards. Work hard to get them out of your organization as quickly as possible.

Activate Team-Member Passion and Purpose

Be careful not to underestimate the significance of passion in coaching your team up. It can be easy to get wrapped up in the objective aspects of work—financial results, sales figures, market research, and statistical models, just to name a few. But when we focus solely on the head, at the expense of the heart, we miss an opportunity to engage with our teammates in a game-changing way. Renowned author and speaker Simon Sinek says that "whether we care to admit it or not, we are not entirely rational beings. If we were, no one would ever fall in love, and no one would ever start a business. Faced with a high probability of failure, no rational person would ever take those risks. But we do. Every day. Because how we feel about something or someone is more powerful than what we think about it or them."

Here is a personal example, which demonstrates the gravitational pull of "passion over logic" in my own life. For as long as I can remember, I have been a die-hard North Carolina Tarheel supporter, or addict, as my wife likes to remind me. While I enjoy all UNC sports, my blood bleeds Carolina blue for Tarheel basketball.

While I am many years removed from my time on campus as a UNC student, and despite the fact I now reside hundreds of miles away from Chapel Hill, I remain as fanatical about the success of the team as ever. Honestly, I am a bit embarrassed (OK, a lot) to admit that during basketball season my emotional state is largely determined by game wins and losses. A major victory, particularly over Duke or NC State, reenergizes my outlook on life, while a gut-wrenching loss sends me into an emotional tailspin for days on end.

The irony of this example is not lost on me. From a purely logical stand-point, my attitude is being largely dictated by the performance of a team of eighteen-to-twenty-two-year-olds who I have neither met nor even spoken to. Other than the fact we share the same alma mater, there is a pretty decent chance we have little else in common. But despite this realization, I still find myself regularly yelling at my television and throwing random objects around the house. Illogical? Absolutely. Emotionally intoxicating? One hundred percent yes! Perhaps I should heed my wife's advice to seek professional help.

Research tells us that people of all generations and backgrounds are increasingly looking for work that has intrinsic emotional value while also providing a defined pathway to continuous development. When it comes to coaching your team members, make every effort to connect with them at a head *and* heart level. It is at this intersection that you will help them discover true purpose and meaning in their work, and you will inspire them to bring their very best to the workplace.

Next Steps on the Pathway-to-Purpose Journey

→ **Collaborate with your senior leadership team to establish formal coaching guidelines for all company managers.** Include expectations around continuous feedback, goal setting, accountability metrics, etc.

→ **In advance of your next leader meeting, ask team members to come prepared to share an example of a former manager that had a positive influence on their career path.** What key attributes did the manager demonstrate that made them so effective?

→ **What behaviors are you simply unwilling to tolerate in your organization?** Are there any active employees who are regularly crossing the line when it comes to unacceptable behavior? If so, what steps will you take to ensure guilty team members clearly understand the ramifications if the issues persist?

→ **Review the traditional views of bosses versus contemporary views of coaches outlined in figure 5.1.** To what extent would a manager-as-coach approach benefit your organization? What actions will you commit to over the next thirty days to improve the effectiveness of your manager population?

Chapter 6

OWNING: DRIVE ACCOUNTABILITY

The unexpected and frightening outbreak of COVID-19 in 2020 affected us all in a multitude of ways. Economic turmoil ensued, with thousands of customer-facing businesses permanently shuttering their doors. Other cornerstones of a free society, including our schools and places of worship, were forced to transition to largely virtual environments. As Americans and global citizens, our resilience and innovative spirit were mightily tested.

Even some of the more pedestrian components of our daily lives were at times turned upside down, with toilet paper shortages, limited dine-in restaurant options, and a lack of televised sports, just to name a few. During the initial weeks of the virus outbreak, the fitness center where I work out closed indefinitely due to spiking coronavirus cases. My one-stop shop for staying fit, complete with basketball court, swimming pool, cardio/weight machines, free weights, and specialized training classes, was no longer available at my beck and call. I desperately needed a plan B.

As fate would have it, a potential solution to my fitness challenge unexpectedly emerged. After the pandemic forced the University of Georgia to temporarily shut down all in-person classes, my daughter Elaina returned home early for summer break to finish the school year remotely. It turned out that Elaina had recently begun jogging regularly near campus with a roommate and was looking for a new exercise partner since she would be stuck at home for some period of time. She enthusiastically suggested that we start running together, but I was very opposed to the idea at first—not because I don't love Elaina dearly or failed to see it as a great father-daughter bonding opportunity. My real reason for such strong resistance?

It is a bit embarrassing to admit, but I actually hate running! I don't just dislike it…I hate it. Drop me on a basketball court or football field, and I will gladly run until I collapse. Heck, over many years I have even gotten relatively comfortable working out on a treadmill. But asking me to run outdoors just for the sake of running? It has about as much appeal as being poked in the eye with a blow poke. Yet despite all of my reservations, I decided to accept Elaina's workout challenge.

It was in the midst of this fitness partnership that I learned some unexpected best practices regarding the art of accountability. Later in the chapter, I will circle back with the specifics, but in the meantime, let's evaluate some fundamentals of accountability to better understand how it can be used as a force for good within your organization.

What Exactly Is Accountability?

According to the online *Merriam-Webster* dictionary, *accountability* is "an obligation or willingness to accept responsibility, or to account for one's actions." Further investigation reveals that the word *obligation* has to do with being morally or legally bound to do something. The whole perception of accountability wrapped together in this context feels a bit constricting and punitive, don't you think? Instead of an emphasis on willingly accepting responsibility for a particular goal or outcome, the more depressing image is that of being forced to do something you have no desire to do.

My personal definition of accountability is simply *doing what you say you will do*. It is a willingness to accept responsibility for your commitments and a refusal to place blame elsewhere when things go south. Accountability is having the courage to show up and step up. Think about it. Look behind the curtain of any successful individual or significant endeavor, and you will discover an environment where accountability is not just tolerated but embraced.

Clearly, one of the primary benefits of accountability is to help us achieve our goals. A recent study conducted by the Association for Talent Development revealed that directly communicating a goal to someone can raise the probability of success to 65 percent. The additional step of conducting a follow-up meeting increases the chances of success to an amazing 95 percent! [1]

Probability of Goal Completion
- **10 percent** if you have an actual idea or goal
- **25 percent** if you consciously decide you will do it
- **40 percent** if you decide when you will do it
- **50 percent** if you plan how you will do it
- **65 percent** if you commit to someone you will do it
- **95 percent** if you have a specific accountability appointment with a person you've committed to

---

FIGURE 6.1

Effective accountability not only fosters goal achievement; it also helps us focus on the aspects of our jobs that are most important. For example, no one is holding me accountable to earn a master certification as a commodities trader. It is simply not a priority for me (nor my boss, thank goodness), so I am therefore not compelled to focus my limited time and energy on something entirely outside my career path! On the other hand, identifying timely, measurable action steps to increase my work performance and effectiveness is absolutely a priority. The same is true for our employees. Without a clearly defined accountability process, team members will become focused on a wide range of disparate tasks that fail to effectively serve the larger corporate strategy.

Distinguish Owners from Renters

If we aspire to build cultures of accountability, we must be willing to hold ourselves accountable to the same performance expectations as our people. Leaders have a fundamental duty to act in the collective best interest of their key stakeholders. In our roles as leaders and coaches, we are called to accept responsibility for both our own performance and the performance of our teams. Of course, this is easy to do when results are favorable. The real challenge is to resist blaming someone or something else when outcomes are poor.

Consider some of the real-world differences between owners and renters. When you are a property owner, you bear full responsibility for property upgrades, maintenance, and repair. You are also accountable for ensuring the mortgage, property taxes, and utilities are paid on time and in full. While you might ultimately entrust some unwanted tasks to external professionals (landscapers, HVAC mechanics, chimney sweeps, etc.), at the end of the day your bear responsibility. In sharp contrast, a renter has a very different point of view regarding liability. If the roof springs a leak or the dishwasher dies, common protocol is to lodge a complaint with the property owner and wait to have the issue resolved for you. Renters delegate responsibility to others. They absolve themselves of any obligation that is not self-inflicted, and depending on the severity of their property complaint, they might even see themselves as a victim of circumstance.

The relationship between owners and renters provides an interesting backdrop when we contemplate the continuum of *personal* accountability. On one end of the continuum are the owners—those individuals who enthusiastically and voluntarily embrace the power of establishing goals and taking responsibility for attaining them. To owners, accountability is a means for continuous improvement; it is a necessary investment in personal development.

On the opposite end of the accountability scale are the renters. Instead of taking responsibility for failed outcomes, renters find solace in shifting liability elsewhere. If you could go inside the renter's head, you would likely hear them ruminating on some variation of the following questions, all in a measured attempt to shift culpability away from themselves:

- Whom can I blame for my inability to reach my goals? *(**blamer** mindset)*

- Why did my boss (or my teammates, the economy, the coronavirus, etc.) have to undermine my opportunity to reach my goals? *(**victim** mindset)*

- When will things ever go my way so that I can realistically reach my goals? *(**procrastinator** mindset)*

Do any of these questions and corresponding mindsets ring familiar? Perhaps you have heard individuals on your own team complain in a similar fashion in the past. Or maybe you have found *yourself* uttering these questions in the midst of a particularly painful failure! If you are personally guilty of the blamer, victim, or procrastinator mindset, hold yourself accountable for changing your ways. If those you lead have developed a propensity to avoid gazing in the mirror, have the courage to coach them through their blind spots. Just as importantly, take time to examine how you and/or your organization may be contributing to the renter mentality.

One reason why holding ourselves accountable can be so challenging is that we live in a world that increasingly endorses and even celebrates looking outside ourselves to justify poor performance and bad behavior. To not accept personal accountability has unfortunately become the socially accepted norm, and we must fight the temptation to allow this dangerous mentality to take root in our workplaces.

Be a Helper, Not a Hammer
Imagine for a moment you are a senior leader for an up-and-coming technology sales company that has just been acquired by a competitor as part of a hostile takeover. Unfortunately, your beloved CEO has been ousted. She built a highly respected and profitable organization based on a collective commitment to performance excellence, continuous learning, and collaborative teamwork. Not surprisingly, there is an elevated sense of uncertainty and angst in the boardroom on this particular day, as you and your teammates wait to hear from your new boss for the first time.

The first few minutes seem to go smoothly enough, as obligatory introductions and small talk help to lighten the mood. Things quickly turn for the worse, however, as the CEO pulls out the P&L statement for the most recent quarter. "I understand that company revenues for Q3 were your best ever," he says in a less-than-enthusiastic tone. "You and your teams must be very proud." After pausing for effect, he continues. "I must confess, however, that I am not at all impressed. Sales are nowhere near where they should and could be, and expenses are completely out of line. I could care less whether this is your top performance in history or not. The numbers are simply not good enough, and they will not be tolerated going forward. Rest assured, I will hold each and every one of you personally accountable for significant improvement. No excuses…Just results!" In that moment, you could have heard a pin drop. It was as if every ounce of oxygen (and hope) had been literally sucked out of the room.

Unfortunately, similar examples of old-school accountability in the workplace are still commonplace today. The story above hearkens back to an age when leaders directed their subordinates with an iron fist, holding firmly to a "might makes right" mentality. Accountability was wielded across all organizational levels as an intimidation tactic, and there was little tolerance for individuals who strayed outside the norm. Employee empowerment and collaboration were foreign concepts. "Just do what you are told, and don't ask any questions!" Naturally, people followed because they had to, not out of a sense of loyalty or respect. With this backdrop in mind, is it any wonder that most people continue to have an overwhelmingly negative reaction to the idea of accountability?

This is a *big* deal. If we are to become leaders worth following, if we are serious about creating world-class cultures, then we have to get accountability right. It requires that we take an honest look at the overarching intent of accountability within our organizations and, just as importantly, how team members experience being held accountable on a daily basis. As in the fictional example above, is accountability a punitive weapon we hold over our people to pound them into submission? Do we use it as a *hammer*? Or, do we instead employ accountability as a *helper* to move them closer to realizing their full potential? Accountability should always be used as a tool to inspire rather than a leash to demoralize.

Leverage Constructive Accountability to Fuel Purpose

Believe it or not, we all desire accountability. As mentioned previously, accountability is a prerequisite for success in business and life because accomplishing anything of significance requires some combination of taking personal responsibility for our own actions and enlisting others to help keep us on task. Author Will Craig notes that "accountability is the glue that bonds commitment to results." I love Craig's metaphor here. Commitment can be very powerful, but over time, it tends to wane, particularly in the presence of conflicting priorities or pain. Adding accountability to the mix forces us to refocus, recommit, and stay the path.

Everybody wants to know how they measure up and where they stand. We crave progress. The most miserable and disengaged employees are often those deprived of any objective means of evaluation. To withhold constructive accountability from our team members is to rob them of a sense of self-worth and empowerment.

Patrick Lencioni writes, "Once we achieve clarity and buy-in, it is then that we have to hold each other accountable for what we sign up to do, for high standards of performance and behavior. And as simple as that sounds, most executives hate to do it, especially when it comes to a peer's behavior."

You can assign tasks, but you cannot force people to be accountable. Accountability is an act of will.
—Unknown

Let's circle back now to the opening section of this chapter. I will outline ten key accountability strategies employed by my daughter to lead me down a performance path I would not have ventured by myself. Remarkably, Elaina implemented each strategy without the prior benefits of any formal business training or practical work experience. We became accountability partners of sorts, but Elaina was without a doubt the lead architect in this arrangement!

Key Accountability Strategies
Strategy 1: Beware of Pushing Too Hard, Too Soon
As I mentioned earlier, Elaina had already developed a consistent jogging regimen prior to her returning home for the summer. She had more endurance than I did early on, so challenging me to run a 5K or half marathon

right out of the gate would have set me up to crash and burn. It would have also increased the likelihood of me pursuing a very different path. Instead, Elaina insisted that we establish achievable performance milestones from the outset.

Calling back to chapter 5, personal growth requires going outside of your comfort zone and entering the zone of learning. In the business world, leaders must become competent at gauging the speed and intensity required to motivate employees to perform at their best. Pushing too hard, too soon can lead to panic zone behaviors like fear and frustration.

People who believe their goals are unrealistic will often simply give up, or they will look elsewhere to place blame. We have an obligation as leaders to ensure the performance metrics assigned to our employees are challenging enough to expand their current capabilities but realistic enough to keep them motivated.

Strategy 2: Establish Objective Measures of Accountability
An important characteristic of accountability is to provide a snapshot of how we are doing. In the process of constructive accountability, both the person accepting responsibility and the one requiring it should be able to evaluate progress performance standards specified in the original agreement. When done effectively, accountability nurtures confidence while eliminating ambiguity.

From the outset, Elaina and I conferred to determine what success should look like, not just at the end of our journey but step-by-step along the way. It would not have been advisable for Elaina to say to me, "Dad, I am going to hold you accountable for becoming a world-class runner before I head back to school!" This assertion would have lacked sufficient objectivity to actually define "world-class runner." Would it mean shaving a specific number of minutes off my current mile time, increasing my long-distance capacity to cover a set number of miles, improving particular aspects of my running form, or something else entirely? You cannot truly hold someone accountable for something in the absence of objective, detailed performance criteria.

In our particular case, Elaina and I committed to achieving twenty-five-to-thirty-minute runs a minimum of three times per week, at an approximate ten-minute-per-mile pace. In addition, I personally committed to completing a company 5K race and to dropping at least eight pounds by the end of the summer. Again, we knew we could not realistically just show up in order to be successful. We therefore established a series of additional subgoals, which allowed us to experience some early victories and ultimately reach our final targets.

Now, for you runners out there, these goals may look pedestrian to you. But for us, accomplishing them (which we did!) represented significant improvement. Regardless, my main point is that in order to determine where you are headed and whether you succeeded, you must first define how success will be measured within the context of your goals. Otherwise, you will have no way of determining whether you won or not.

Strategy 3: Avoid Shame or Intimidation as an Accountability Tactic
To this point in the book, we have clearly established that a command-and-control leadership style is less acceptable and effective than at any other time in history. Attempting to leverage shame or intimidation as a means to garner improved performance is not a sustainable business strategy in the modern-day workplace. Nothing destroys human passion and ingenuity like the hammer mentality mentioned previously. More than ever, people have options when it comes to their careers. Forward-thinking organizations that treat their employees like valued business partners rather than disposable assets become the undisputed employers of choice, thus attracting the very best and brightest talent available.

In the same way, I would *not* have found it intrinsically motivating during my workouts to have Elaina nipping at my heels on an electric scooter, yelling for me to pick up the pace and to stop acting like a pathetic loser! Instead, like all purpose-driven leaders, she became a primary source of encouragement and inspiration. I hope that I was able to do the same for her!

Strategy 4: Stay in the Game and Remain Connected
One of the greatest mistakes leaders can make when it comes to accountability is to first institute employee work expectations and then not provide ample support to help guide team members along the performance journey.

This mistake is essentially the antithesis of a micromanager, who makes it their life mission to scrutinize your every move.

The "macro-manager," by contrast, can be just as frustrating and problematic to deal with. They lead from afar and refuse to get involved in the day-to-day. This arrangement might work fine in a low-stakes environment but not so much when the results employees are liable for are in significant jeopardy and your boss (the one who is holding your feet to the fire) is perpetually missing in action. Think of the college professor who on the first day of class goes into great detail regarding the learning content their students are responsible for mastering by semester's end only to regularly cancel classes, provide no supplemental reading material, and offer no review sessions leading up to the dreaded five-hour final exam.

Do not place massive responsibilities on others and then withhold your support or input. Your team members will eventually become embittered and demotivated. Thank goodness Elaina did not proclaim she would be holding me accountable for a challenging goal yet fail to provide any direction on how to properly pursue it. We are obligated in our leadership roles to coach our teammates up throughout the process. Merely setting expectations and walking away is a setup for frustration and underperformance. Our people need to know that we have their backs and that we are fully invested in helping them achieve their goals.

Strategy 5: Paint an Honest Picture (as Best You Can) of the Road Ahead
Many years ago, at the urging of my oldest daughter, Madalyn, I reluctantly ordered an iPod Classic off Craigslist. For those of you who might not remember (or had not been born), the iPod was a portable media player introduced by Apple in the early 2000s. Think of it as a precursor to today's smartphone in terms of music storage, allowing users to house thousands of songs on a single device. The advertised price for this brand-new device was more than half off retail, so I was cautiously optimistic. I arrived at the agreed-upon pickup location and actually found the seller to be very credible. The iPod appeared to be totally undisturbed, and it was still in its original packaging. Call me naive, but I decided to proceed with the transaction.

Of course, the whole thing ended up being a total fabrication. After arriving home, I excitedly pulled the device out of the packaging, turned it on, and was greeted with the following screen message: "Congratulations IDIOT! You have been punked." No more than ten seconds later, the device went dark...permanently. To this day, the iPod lies in a storage bin at my home, reminding me that things of real value are rarely earned through taking shortcuts or an unwillingness to pay the necessary price.

Nobody enjoys being sold a pack of lies when making a purchase. In the same way, employees want to know the unvarnished truth with regard to expectations set by their supervisors. Resist the temptation to portray the road ahead as a walk in the park when you know it will likely be fraught with landmines. Do not sugarcoat reality in an effort to protect team-member feelings or to avoid overwhelming them. Be a straight shooter, but at the same time, let them know you will be there to help support and guide them throughout the process.

In the case of our exercise commitments, Elaina and I both knew we would be stretching ourselves to successfully reach our exercise goals. Neither of us pretended it was going to be easy. We were very aware of what we were getting ourselves into, but in our minds, the eventual benefits of seeing it through would far exceed any short-term pain.

> It is not when things come easily that we appreciate them,
> but when we have to work hard for them, or when they
> are hard to get, that those things have greater value to us.
> —Simon Sinek

Strategy 6: Remember—Trust Is Foundational
Do not expect your team members to embrace personal accountability in the absence of foundational trust. As we discovered in the Project Aristotle research conducted by Google and highlighted in chapter 4, the number one attribute found to be universally present in high-performing teams is a sense of psychological safety. To enthusiastically accept responsibility for

their job performance, employees must have full confidence that they can bring their unvarnished selves to work each day without fear of rejection or reprisal. In his book *Leaders Eat Last*, Simon Sinek refers to this state as the "circle of safety." He notes that engendering trust within organizational cultures is much more than merely telling the truth in a traditional sense. While honesty is essential to any enterprise, it will not differentiate your organization from the many others who also operate in an ethical fashion.[2]

Circles of safety do not occur by chance. They are the result of leaders who foster company environments where diversity of thought is embraced, failure is not final, and caring for your teammates is nonnegotiable. Leaders are not truly leaders until they have earned the trust of those they lead. And trusting your manager requires a belief that he cares about you not just as an employee but also as a fellow human being. We all want to know that those we are accountable to have our best interest in mind. The old Teddy Roosevelt adage is so true: "No one cares how much you know until they know how much you care."

By virtue of our father-daughter relationship, Elaina and I have developed a very strong bond of trust over the course of many years. Fortunately, issues of trust did not come into play with regard to our workout commitments. However, this will not always be the case in the corporate world. Trust is a baseline requirement for any constructive accountability partnership.

> Accountability is a two-way street. As a leader, you want to know that you can count on people to do what they said they would do. Likewise, your colleagues want to know that they can count on you as the leader to do what you have promised them.
> —Greg Bustin

Strategy 7: Encourage Performance Excellence, Not Perfectionism
Several years ago, I had a participant in one of my leadership development seminars named Lizzie (not her real name), who complained that her boss

had "a serious case of the shoulds." Thinking this must be in reference to some sort of obscure physical ailment, I probed for further explanation. It turns out that Lizzie's supervisor had a habit of focusing on her perceived inadequacies by pointing out things she *should* be doing differently. "You should never attempt to do that without checking with me first. You should listen better to my instructions next time. You should know better than that by now." Lizzie, now on the verge of tears, further shared that the condescending nature of the feedback left her in constant fear of the next criticism. "I feel like I can't do anything right anymore," Lizzie said. "I've lost complete confidence in my abilities."

During the lunch break, I had the opportunity to sit with Lizzie and discuss her situation in greater detail. I asked Lizzie to consider her manager's motivation and whether she believed he had positive intentions when correcting her. Lizzie thought for a moment and then noted that she did think he meant well. She also agreed that her leader probably did not realize his feedback style was causing her such distress. With this factor in mind, I encouraged Lizzie to schedule time with her manager to honestly share her feelings. She agreed to do it while admitting that the prospect of doing so made her extremely anxious.

Before heading back for the afternoon session, I asked Lizzie if she felt a constant urge to be the perfect wife, mother, friend, employee, etc. As her eyes misted over, Lizzie nodded her head in agreement. In that moment, I shared with Lizzie my personal struggles with perfectionism and how critical it was for us to be compassionate with ourselves in the midst of our imperfections. Instead of being held hostage by the bonds of perfectionism, I said, we can be inspired by our pursuit of excellence. Regardless of the eventual meeting outcome with her boss, Lizzie made a promise to herself that day to always try to push forward rather than fall backward. While she may have very limited control of how the meeting turned out, she had complete control over her subsequent reaction and future behavior.

Leaders have an obligation to guide both themselves and their people in pursuit of constant improvement, not faultless performance. Fixating on past mistakes (shoulds) just further fuels the flames of perfectionism and enslaves everyone in its path. Exceptional cultures pursue excellence and avoid perfectionism.

Elaina and I both consider ourselves to be "recovering perfectionists," so we understand the real-world pitfalls of trying to operate within a zero-defect construct. As such, we were vigilant about not beating each other nor ourselves up along the way. Mutual accountability, particularly in this scenario, proved to be invaluable.

Strategy 8: Resist Doing the Work for Them

I have found that many business leaders struggle with delegating critical job responsibilities to their employees. It appears the popular saying has become ingrained in our leadership ethos: "If you want something done right, you have to do it yourself!" But beware, this mindset is dangerous on a number of levels.

By stepping in to do their work for them, leaders are undermining employee growth and development. Our workers fail to receive valuable experience, which can have major implications for the trajectory of their careers. The long-term impacts of this practice are similar in many respects to what is happening with great frequency today in parent-child relationships. Parents are shielding their kids from assuming personal responsibility in areas that would have traditionally been unthinkable. For example, it is not uncommon for helicopter parents to personally write their middle and high schoolers' essays or term papers. Even more startling, human resource professionals report that a growing number of parents actually sit in on their adult children's job interviews. Think about that. Would you want to hire a recent college graduate who showed up for a job interview with one of their parents in tow? Just as parents put their children's futures at risk by not empowering them to take responsibility for their own battles, we do the same to our employees when we rob them of the chance to figure things out on their own. By assuming responsibility for tasks we have already delegated to others, our credibility will suffer. Team-member passion and creativity will also erode as our employees begin to question if our actions reflect a lack of confidence in their capabilities.

Fortunately for Elaina, stepping in to run on my behalf was not a viable option as I would accrue none of the benefits of exercising on my own!

Strategy 9: Point Out the Bad Stuff, Even When It Feels Uncomfortable
Have you ever been around people who constantly tell you what you want to hear rather than what you need to hear? While often well intentioned, leaders must be careful to avoid going down this path with their employees. I used to be a big fan of *American Idol*, the popular singing competition show on television. During the early years of the program, judge Simon Cowell became famous for his no-nonsense approach to participant feedback. While some might have questioned the general tone and veracity of his feedback, Cowell was unwavering in both his praise and criticism. He believed that these aspiring singers, who in many cases had already dedicated huge chunks of their lives to pursuing their musical dreams, deserved to know the cold, hard truth—regardless of how awkward it might be for Cowell to deliver or how painful it might be for the contestants to receive.

Don't shirk your responsibility to call your people out when they are underperforming or trending in the wrong direction. Though we should always be respectful, being nice to avoid conflict is not helpful. Leaders have an obligation to be genuine and courageous with their performance feedback. Letting things slide in the short term may often be the easier option, but it is never in our best interest or in the best interest of the people we lead.

On more than one occasion, Elaina had to remind me not to allow outside influences like heat, fatigue, or competing priorities to distract me from my goals. While her feedback approach is very different from Simon Cowell's approach, she was just as effective at communicating what I needed to hear.

Strategy 10: Remember to Incorporate Purpose into Accountability Conversations
Do not overlook the opportunity to communicate the larger why behind assigned accountability metrics. Based on her research regarding the crisis of accountability in today's workforce, transformational leader Anne Loehr reports that 93 percent of employees do not even understand what their organization is trying to accomplish, thus preventing them from aligning

corporate mission and key business objectives with their own job functions. Furthermore, 84 percent of workers describe themselves "as 'trying but failing' or 'avoiding' accountability, even when employees know what to fix."[3]

As emphasized throughout this book, aligning job responsibilities with organizational and individual purpose is essential to cultivating exceptional cultures. People are much more likely to embrace personal accountability when they see that their efforts serve a greater purpose. The next time you sit down with each of your employees to review their specific performance goals and related progress, make sure they can articulate how their personal efforts are contributing to the organization's higher calling. Coach them up where any gaps exist. In the event you also struggle to make the connection between mission and goals, consider whether it might be time to either tweak or change certain ones.

I identified my greater purpose in accepting Elaina's running challenge right away. For me, it was not so much about looking more buff or aspiring to become a marathon runner (remember, I hate running). My deeper why was, and is, to be alive and healthy enough to walk my daughters down the aisle, to spend quality time with my grandkids, to actively volunteer in my church and local community, and to travel with my wife to fun and exciting places. When things got tough over the summer, when I found myself looking for an excuse to opt out of my running commitments, Elaina always managed to redirect me toward the bigger life picture.

Final Thoughts
Remember Everybody Is Accountable to Somebody
Though you may never have taken the time to consider it, at the end of the day, *everybody is accountable to somebody*. A politician is accountable to their constituents. A pastor or priest is accountable to their congregation. An employee is accountable to their supervisor. Even a CEO or owner is accountable to their board of directors and shareholders. Personal and collective responsibility must be alive and well across all business levels; otherwise, organizations become susceptible to a slow burn and, in some extreme cases, an abrupt implosion. You might recall from chapter 3 the account of former American energy company Enron, which collapsed in

large part because of a CEO and senior leadership team that refused to hold themselves accountable for company values they personally conceived and subsequently demanded that their workforce obey.

Next Steps on the Pathway-to-Purpose Journey

→ **Ask yourself the following questions.** In my organization, is accountability being leveraged more as a fear tactic or a pathway to excellence? Do employees typically embrace accountability or run from it? What steps can our leadership team take to fully shift perceptions of accountability from that of a hammer to a helper?

→ **Review the ten accountability strategies outlined in this chapter.** Pick at least two strategies that you consider areas of opportunity in your leadership role. What steps will you take to address them going forward? Ask a fellow leader to hold you accountable for improvement.

→ **To what extent is an attitude of victimization used as an excuse for poor performance within your organization?** Does it permeate your leadership ranks, or even apply to the way others perceive you at times? What steps will you take to transform victim-based mindsets within the enterprise?

→ **Would your direct reports say you are more of a "helper" or a "hammer?"** What steps could you take to move more towards the "helper" side?

Chapter 7

RECOGNIZING: CELEBRATE ACHIEVEMENT

In chapter 6, we discussed accountability, which is the first key component of performance excellence. We learned that high performers view accountability as a pathway to continuous improvement, particularly when applied in a constructive and inspirational manner. In this chapter we'll evaluate the fundamental companion to accountability: *recognition*.

On the surface, accountability and recognition may appear to be total opposites. In reality, however, accountability and recognition are two sides of the same coin, *if* they are properly employed. Recognition is at the heart of our willingness to be held responsible. As high performers, we voluntarily accept ownership for our commitments because we yearn for progress and the resulting fruits of success. But we also long for external validation that our efforts are praiseworthy and that they have perceived value outside of ourselves.

So how do accountability and recognition relate to one another? My friend and former colleague Richard Tiller once explained it to me this way: "Accountability without recognition is demoralizing, and recognition without accountability is hollow."

Think about it. Old-school accountability, when used as a hammer to pound employees into submission, is very discouraging. Extract all traces of praise or recognition, and it will crush the human spirit, sucking the life out of your people and reducing them to a shell of their God-given potential. With this reality in mind, I urge each of you to evaluate where you currently fall on the accountability/recognition scale. If your style is heavily weighted toward the accountability side, take steps today to move the pendulum more towards recognition. Begin to acknowledge and call out exceptional performance when you see it, and exercise accountability as a helper, not a hammer.

The opposite extreme is demonstrated by leaders who go out of their way to continuously praise and recognize their people yet fail to define for them what excellence truly looks like. The old cliché holds true: "You can't manage what you can't measure." Without clear performance metrics, accountability is nothing more than smoke and mirrors. And as a result, recognition will fall short of the intended impact. Instead of inspiring your team to repeat and improve upon sought-after behaviors, they will be left with a watered-down version of recognition that feels disingenuous or even contrived. In the absence of objective accountability, your people will begin to view recognition (financial incentives, office perks, verbal praise, etc.) as an entitlement and not a privilege. If your leadership scales are tipping too far on the recognition side, make sure to counterbalance the performance equation by infusing clear and achievable goals into your talent management system.

In summary, great leaders are able to balance task focus (getting things done) with people focus (inspiring, developing, and empowering others). Maximizing talent and performance demands a thoughtful blend of both accountability and recognition.

Making the Case for Recognition

Employee recognition was not widely considered a meaningful performance enhancer until the early part of the twentieth century. The prevailing mindset of company brass prior to this time was that employees should be thankful to have a job…period. Consequently, subordinates were expected to cheerfully carry out their job duties without protest or expectation of some external validation. Receiving a paycheck was thought to be sufficient recognition. Alas, work was, by and large, a means to an end. Little intrinsic value was generally found in one's work, and therefore limited motivation existed to stir the collective passion of a team. Views regarding workplace recognition have fortunately continued to progress over the past several decades, as we continue to understand how reward and recognition can be used as a force for good.

So what is the underlying objective of reward and recognition initiatives in the workplace, and why does *every* irresistible culture place such significant emphasis on celebrating the outstanding efforts of employees? They do it because treating others with dignity and respect is the honorable thing to do. Effective recognition serves to validate not just that their *work* matters but that *they* matter as well. When team members feel valued, their satisfaction and productivity levels soar, and they are motivated to give more of themselves for a bigger cause. So, while authentic-based recognition (as opposed to manipulation) is definitely a kind and noble act, it is also a powerful tool to reinforce actions that fuel organizational success.

A growing body of research in the area of employee recognition provides interesting insights on the topic. Here are several key points to consider:

- Leaders have a significantly overinflated level of confidence in the effectiveness of their recognition efforts.
  - Sixty-seven percent of managers believe they are "above average" at appreciating great work, while only 23 percent of employees agree.[1]
- Though people may be wired differently when it comes to motivation, *everyone* wants to be appreciated.
  - Four in five employees (81 percent) say they are motivated to work harder when their boss shows appreciation for their work.[2]
- Recognition is a major determinant of employee retention. Forms of reward and recognition do not have to be elaborate or even expensive, but they do have to be timely and sincere.
  - More than half (53 percent) of employees report they would stay longer at their company if they felt more appreciation from their boss.[3]
- A large percentage of the workforce is highly motivated by nonmonetary forms of recognition that are communicated *publicly*, often to even higher levels than financial recognition provided privately.

- ° Nearly one-third (30 percent) of employees would rather be recognized for their work accomplishments in a company-wide email from a company executive than to receive a monetary bonus of $500 that is not openly publicized by a superior to their coworkers.[4]
- The efficacy and frequency of positive recognition in the workplace is highly correlated to employee job satisfaction.
  - ° Ninety-four percent of employees who receive positive recognition from a supervisor for their performance "daily or more often" are either satisfied or very satisfied with their current job, while just 43 percent of employees recognized by a supervisor "less than a few times a year" are satisfied or very satisfied.[5]

People will die for the ribbon.
—Napoleon

Understand the True Determinants of Motivation

While leading quality and customer experience initiatives with Ritz-Carlton, I had the occasion to deal with some highly demanding hotel guests. Expectations, particularly at some of the more opulent locales, were sky-high, which is understandable given the amount of money guests shell out for the Ritz-Carlton experience. I learned early on that certain service elements, even when executed to perfection, did not, in and of themselves, fuel guest satisfaction. But those same elements, when executed poorly, would drive guests away from the hotel and potentially the Ritz brand forever.

By way of example, I *never* once had a customer approach me to rave that their guest room was free of crumbs or dust bunnies. Neither did I encounter a single such shout-out while reviewing thousands of guest survey comments during my years at the Ritz. It just didn't happen! The absence of defects in the luxury hotel business does not earn the property or company any psychological brownie points. Defect-free experiences are a minimum standard: mere table steaks. But fail to meet the basics, and major dissatisfaction is sure to ensue!

Research in the realm of employee recognition and motivation provides similar insights when it comes to factors of dissatisfaction. Frederick Herzberg was an American clinical psychologist and professor of management at the University of Utah. His 1968 *Harvard Business Review* essay "One More Time: How Do You Motivate Employees?" is the most requested article in the publication's history. Herzberg is best known for introducing the motivator-hygiene theory. The theory was derived from extensive interviews he conducted with employees in the 1950s to better understand which environmental attributes resulted in positive job perceptions and which led to negative ones. Herzberg's research found that what he called "hygiene factors," which include things like salary, working conditions, and company policies, were crucial for avoiding job *dissatisfaction*, but they had minimal impact on job *satisfaction*. This is akin to the customer service scenario above in which hotel guests don't experience measurable satisfaction when, say, their television works properly, but they become very frustrated when it is inoperable!

In contrast to dissatisfaction, job satisfaction, according to Herzberg, is contingent on higher-level "motivator factors" like autonomy, opportunities for personal growth, and finding pleasure in the work itself. Organizations hoping to boost employee performance by focusing on hygiene factors might see a temporary performance lift but not a sustainable one. Herzberg frequently referred to hygiene elements as KITA factors—his acronym for "kick in the A$$." In this context, KITA is the process of providing either incentives or the threat of punishment to cause someone to behave in a certain way. Herzberg argued that these factors provide only short-run success because the motivator factors that determine satisfaction are largely internal in nature.[6]

Identify Key Motivational Operating Systems
In his highly acclaimed and best-selling book *Drive: The Surprising Truth about What Motivates Us*, Daniel Pink further expounds upon the motivation work of Frederick Herzberg, Douglas McGregor, Peter Drucker, and others.

Pink outlines three motivational operating systems, or sets of assumptions, about how the world works and how humans behave. He refers to them, quite simply, as Motivation 1.0, 2.0, and 3.0. Motivation 1.0 dates back to the beginning of human life and deals with our basic survival instincts.[7] People are immediately motivated when their existence is threatened. If you come face-to-face in the wilderness with a hungry grizzly bear, your singular goal is to live to tell about it. Nothing else matters in that moment. It is a drive about as primal and simplistic as it gets!

The Motivation 2.0 operating system extends beyond basic survival and focuses heavily on carrot-and-stick methodologies. It presumes that people are primarily motivated by reward and punishment. In fact, most organizations today adhere to this philosophy and its assumption that the way to improve performance and drive desired behaviors is to reward the good and punish the bad. In the words of Pink:

> Despite its greater sophistication and higher aspirations [over Motivation 1.0], Motivation 2.0 still wasn't exactly enno-bling. It suggested that, in the end, human beings aren't much different than livestock—that the way to get us mov-ing in the right direction is by dangling a crunchier carrot or wielding a sharper stick. But what this operating system lacked in enlightenment, it made up for in effectiveness. It worked well—extremely well. Until it didn't.

Pink argues that Motivation 2.0 has become increasingly ineffective in modern society, largely because the nature of our work has shifted. On the whole, job roles are now much more *heuristic* (complex and requiring creative thought) than *algorithmic* (mechanistic and requiring little thought). By way of illustration, job tasks such as stocking shelves, delivering packages, or writing computer code would largely be considered algorithmic because they require that a specific set of rules be followed to reach an expected outcome. In contrast, working as a graphic designer, crafting a new sales presentation, or developing a new smartphone app would be heuristic in nature due to the more creative, right-brained task demands. My youngest daughter, Juliana, falls in the heuristic camp. She is extremely imaginative and artistic, seeing the world as her tapestry to transform "blank slate" concepts into inspiring masterpieces.

Research conducted by consulting firm McKinsey & Co. reveals that 70 percent of job growth in the United States now comes from heuristic work.[8] The problem with the carrot-and-stick approach within largely heuristic job roles is that it can actually be demotivating over time. One explanation for this phenomenon is that jobs requiring greater creativity and complexity are more enjoyable. This runs counter to the outdated Motivation 2.0 belief that work is unpleasant and boring and therefore employees must be externally motivated/manipulated in order to perform at acceptable levels.

According to Pink, Motivation 3.0 is the operational upgrade desperately needed for the modern world. It assumes humans have a third drive fueled from *within* to continuously grow and make a positive difference in life. Whereas Motivation 2.0 is largely based on external/hygiene factors like pay raises and job perks, Motivation 3.0 is driven by internal/motivator dynamics like the desire for greater job autonomy and a yearning for higher purpose.[9]

The implications of motivation-based discoveries are substantial when it comes to organizational reward and recognition efforts. For example, let's take a closer look at the long-held belief that money is the mother of all recognition tools in the workplace. I have often wondered what it would feel like to work on a factory assembly line, mindlessly pumping out some sort of widget on a factory floor day after day. It is a highly algorithmic work role. No doubt, some people enjoy this type of career and have made a very good living at it. It is an honorable and necessary profession. But for me personally, I feel certain that disillusionment and apathy would creep into my mindset, even if I were handsomely compensated to perform the role. Now, I like money as much as the next person, but in this scenario, I would much rather do something that inspires me and makes me feel alive, even if it means earning significantly less money. How about you? Given the choice of one or the other, would you go with more money or more meaning?

As it turns out, a growing number of people are choosing more meaning. In a recent job study conducted by Jobvite, a major software and recruiting company, one-third of respondents indicated they would be willing to take a 10 percent pay cut for a job they are passionate about and that is in greater alignment with their goals, while another study from the Hays organization revealed that 71 percent of respondents would take a pay cut for the ideal job.[10] Consider the mindset of the exploding millennial generation, which by 2025 will comprise 75 percent of the global workforce.[11] According to a 2018 study conducted by Udemy, learning and development opportunities (42 percent) trailed only health care offerings (48 percent) as the employee benefit millennials consider most important when deciding where they will work. Likewise, 67 percent of millennials say they would leave their current job if it did not include professional development opportunities.[12]

Again, money is a minimum requirement for entrance into the talent game, and it must at least be commensurate with the financial incentives being offered by your competitors. But using compensation as a primary recognition strategy can become a dangerously slippery slope if you seek long-term employee engagement.

Be an Encouragement

Given that the most powerful type of motivation (à la Motivation 3.0) is most often experienced from within, should additional externally based recognition even be utilized? The answer is unequivocally yes, particularly if the recognition includes things like words of affirmation or rewarding deserving employees with new opportunities or experiences. Consider the following true story:

In an old episode of the wildly popular radio show *The Rest of the Story*, broadcaster Paul Harvey tells an account of Stevie Morris and his life-altering encounter with a Detroit schoolteacher. Following the escape of the class pet mouse one day, Stevie's teacher enlisted his help to track it down, and she praised Stevie effusively after he successfully completed the mission. The teacher knew that Stevie had a unique skill that no one else in the entire school possessed. He was gifted with a remarkable set of ears to compensate for his unseeing eyes.

Sadly, this would be one of the few times in Stevie's early childhood years that he was singled out for any type of recognition. Many years later, Stevie reported that his teacher's small act of kindness ultimately changed the trajectory of his life. The young man would continue to perfect his gift of hearing, and he refused to allow blindness to undermine his dreams. Armed with a spirit of gratitude and dogged determination to make something of himself, Stevie Morris—you may know him as Stevie Wonder—would go on to become one of the most famous singers and songwriters in entertainment history.

When it comes to recognition, sometimes the seemingly inconsequential things, such as simple words of affirmation or a handwritten note of appreciation, can make a monumental difference. And in cases like Stevie Wonder, external acknowledgment can often fuel the internal fire necessary to keep someone's hope alive. I love the following line, which is credited to author and motivational speaker Leo Buscaglia: "Too often we underestimate the power of a touch, a smile, a kind word, a listening ear, an honest compliment, or the smallest act of caring, all of which have the potential to turn a life around."

Leverage External Methods to Fuel Intrinsic Motivation

When you love what you do, extrinsic rewards such as
wealth and power become less motivational. You begin to
orient to intrinsic motivators such as meaning,
integrity, love, and learning.

The quote above is taken from Robert Quinn's best-selling book *The Economics of Higher Purpose*. His comments further clarify that intrinsic motivators most appeal to individuals who view their work as a noble, higher calling, while typical external motivators, like money and perks, appeal to those who experience work in a mundane *Groundhog Day* kind of way. Like the Stevie Morris/Wonder example, it is possible to design reward and recognition strategies that fuel greater intrinsic motivation in the workplace.

In his best-selling book *Outliers*, Malcolm Gladwell highlights three specific conditions necessary for our work to be truly satisfying: complexity, autonomy, and linking effort/reward.[13] Let's unpack each of these now.

Complexity

The first quality has to do with the complexity of the job role. Even those of us who enjoy high doses of simplicity in our lives would potentially struggle in an immensely predictable, never-changing work environment (see my earlier example of an assembly-line worker). Boredom and complacency can often creep in, which can lead to your people deciding to quit and leave or, worse yet, quit and stay. Job complexity, on the other hand, implies the journey will not be easy, that there will be significant challenge along the way. As humans, we know that personal growth and development require a willingness to extend beyond what is comfortable. True job satisfaction does not come from starting out with all the answers. It comes from working through trials and uncertainties along the way and making it through to the other side invigorated that our accomplishment was wholly earned. In our role as leaders, the onus is squarely on us to provide meaningful work opportunities for our people. Though every job contains certain humdrum requirements that simply have to be done, we must constantly assess the talent landscape to ensure our employees are being properly motivated and inspired. By rewarding deserving team members with increasingly challenging projects and tasks, we demonstrate our commitment to their career progression.

Autonomy

The second attribute necessary to fuel meaningful work is autonomy. No one likes to be micromanaged. Hovering over your employees and constantly telling them what to do, how to do it, and when to do it creates frustration and distrust. It erodes morale and motivation. The best managers/coaches make sure their team members have been given proper training and have the best resources and tools required to excel. Then the manager gets out of the way and allows the team to thrive while continuing to offer needed support and direction along the way. Autonomy is characterized by a willingness to entrust your high performers to make decisions that are in the best interest of the organization and your key stakeholders.

Take Ritz-Carlton Service Value #3, which states that all employees are "empowered to create unique, memorable and personal experiences for their guests." The fact that every individual within the Ritz organization, from the dishwasher to the valet attendant, is entrusted to spend up to $2,500 at any time to recover a disgruntled customer, further illustrates the company's commitment to entrusting its people to do the right thing. With autonomy, of course, comes responsibility. On the whole, Ritz employees who are given autonomy will take great care not to abuse the privilege, but in the rare event an employee recovery effort is questioned, managers are trained to coach for improvement without dashing team-member morale. Regardless of the industry or institution, workers want to know they have the personal authority to positively impact the enterprise and not just be a cog in the wheel. As my friend Chip Bell is fond of saying, "Empowerment is not about unlimited license. It's about responsible freedom."

How are you and your colleagues creating opportunities for increased autonomy within the ranks of deserving employees? What steps can be taken to widen their net of responsibility while at the same time fueling their desire for growth? Recognition extended through the gift of empowerment is both a powerful motivator and performance enhancer.

People do their best work when they know they're going to be given credit for their contribution. So there has to be a certain amount of autonomy in people's work so they can contribute without reservation...And when creative, self-referenced people do have autonomy, they have the incentive, the energy, and the enthusiasm to do their best. They're proud of their accomplishments and love being given credit for their contributions.
—Dan Pink

The Connection Between Effort and Reward

Former basketball star Kobe Bryant is widely regarded as one of the great-est basketball players in NBA history. Over the course of his twenty-year career with the Los Angeles Lakers, Bryant compiled an amazing resume of accomplishments: five NBA world championships, fifteen All-Star Game appearances, four All-Star Game MVP awards, two NBA Finals MVP awards, and a regular-season MVP award. He was supremely gifted athleti-cally, as evidenced by his superior speed, hand-eye coordination, and leap-ing ability. But practically all athletes at the professional level are endowed with tons of raw athletic talent. What separated Bryant from his basketball contemporaries, however, was his indomitable passion for excellence and his determination to outwork everyone else in order to achieve his dreams. His work habits on the court, in the gym, and in the film room were the stuff of legend.

Bryant fully exemplified the third quality required for a satisfying vo-cation, which is embracing the *connection between effort and reward*. He understood that mere giftedness wasn't sufficient for achieving greatness. True greatness demands an unrelenting commitment to continuous improve-ment, little by little, day after day. It's simple cause and effect. But as we all know, *simple* does not always equate to *easy*.

In an interview immediately following the final game of his illustrious career, Bryant was asked how he wanted to be remembered. His response spoke volumes about the satisfaction he drew from the effort and reward connection: "I want to be remembered as a talented overachiever, someone who was blessed with talent, but worked as if he had none."

If we want meaning in our work, an awareness that good things come from great effort is essential. Leaders have a unique opportunity to highlight and reinforce the importance of the performance struggle when coaching their people. In a call back to chapter 4, heralded psychologist and Stanford professor Carol Dweck says we should avoid praising natural intelligence or talent but instead focus on praising resilience and work ethic. Though the passage I have quoted below refers to some of Dweck's findings in aca-demia, she makes it clear throughout her mindset research that employees also flourish in an environment that recognizes effort over natural ability:

The difference in approach may seem subtle, but the impact is anything but subtle. Look at the following two recognition statements:

Statement #1: Congratulations, Johnny! You are so brilliant. Great job delivering such an impressive sales presentation today.

Statement #2: Congratulations, Johnny! Your hard work and determination sure did pay off. Great job delivering such an impressive sales presentation today.

The first statement validates Johnny for his natural smarts, while the second one focuses on Johnny's overall grit to bring about the desired outcome. Why does any of this matter? Think about it. Based on Statement #1, Johnny's potential as a presenter is fully baked. If another future presentation were to play out less favorably, Johnny's psychological outlook for improvement would be hopelessly fatalistic. From this point of view, there would be no legitimate reason to even try.

But with Statement #2, success is the direct result of Johnny's effort and determination, both of which are entirely in his control. If Johnny is dissatisfied with the outcome of a subsequent presentation, he simply needs to assess what went wrong, and make the necessary changes going forward.

...We can praise wisely, not praising intelligence or talent. That has failed. Don't do that anymore. But praising the process that kids engage in: their effort, their strategies, their focus, their perseverance, their improvement. This process of praise creates kids who are hardy and resilient.

Incorporate Micro-recognition Strategies
In contrast to more formalized recognition programs that tend to be complex and are driven with a top-down approach, *micro-recognition* is very flexible in nature and has few if any barriers for participation. Recognition is dispensed and received from all directions on a frequent and largely informal basis through social praise. Here is an example of a micro-recognition-based strategy that I have seen work very well.

During my tenure with HomeBanc Mortgage Corporation, I oversaw the design and deployment of a recognition program called "Gotcha!" As the name implies, employees were encouraged to "catch" a fellow colleague doing something outstanding and to honor them with a handwritten Gotcha! card. Recipients were invited to provide a copy of their card to human resources for their personnel file and the opportunity to be included in a monthly drawing for cool prizes. I was frankly shocked to observe the personal impact the program had on employees at all organizational levels. A particular employee comes to mind who began to weep uncontrollably after receiving a Gotcha! card from a coworker. The recipient, who had just recently joined the organization, shared that this was the first time in her career someone had taken the time to write a personal note validating her work. Over time, receiving a Gotcha! card became a sort of badge of honor at HomeBanc, with employees proudly posting them in workspaces and offices throughout each facility. A number of respected technology vendors, such as Fond and Workhuman, now specialize in delivering similar online recognition programs.

Another example of micro-recognition (with some more formal elements) has been used for many years at Ritz-Carlton. It's called "Lightning Strikes," and it is a departmental-based slush fund of sorts for managers to provide modest, in-the-moment cash awards for deserving hotel employees. As we covered earlier, monetary recognition has been found to have limited (and in some cases negative) impact on recipient performance, *unless* it is rewarded unexpectedly, à la programs like Lightning Strikes. In these scenarios, motivation and subsequent performance tend to rise precipitously.

Micro-recognition can be as simple as a quick email or verbal affirmation—"Thanks, Tina for your great advice on the Trubisky file. You are a true rock star!" As long as the recognition provided is sincere, personalized, and delivered in a timely fashion, the impacts on team-member morale and performance can be far-reaching.

> There are two things people want more than sex and money—recognition and praise.
> —Mary Kay Ashe

Invest in Formal Recognition

Recognition efforts should strategically link to the attainment and reinforcement of clearly defined objectives and core values. Recognizing mediocre performance will only serve to beget more mediocre performance. Focus on recognizing and celebrating employee behaviors that tightly align with your organizational culture imperatives versus those that will just maintain the status quo. For example, if your company's chief point of strategic differentiation is delivering world-class service, then institute formal recognition programs and processes that reinforce service excellence.

At one of my former employers, a highly respected residential mortgage company consistently ranked among *Fortune* magazine's Best Places to Work, we introduced the Ron Hicks Customer Service Award, named after a former exceptional colleague who passed away suddenly following a tragic car wreck. Hicks epitomized the company's belief that long-term business success begins and ends with delivering exemplary customer service. Employees were encouraged to nominate fellow colleagues who demonstrated specific acts of service heroism.

A committee of peers reviewed each nomination on a monthly basis, with a winner and runner-up receiving a significant cash prize and being verbally recognized in front of all their peers. As the final climax to the company's elaborate annual meeting, each monthly winner was invited onstage to spin a prize wheel. The grand prize for one lucky spinner was a five-day, all-expenses-paid trip for two to a domestic destination of their choice.

Over the years, I have seen a number of highly successful recognition programs designed in the same vein as Ron Hicks. The best ones emphasize and reinforce key company priorities such as innovation, productivity, employee engagement, problem-solving, or community impact. They also do an excellent job of wildly celebrating their culture heroes in a way that makes everyone else want to follow suit!

Final Thoughts
Harness the Power of Story
Another benefit of consistent and public recognition centered on desired performance behaviors is the clarity it engenders among the ranks of your enterprise. Simply encouraging your team to provide great service, asking them to be innovative, or telling them to collaborate effectively does not provide the specificity necessary to execute these directives in a real-world manner. It would be like an athletic coach telling his team to go out and win the game but not providing them with the training and instruction needed to actually make winning a real possibility.

One of the best ways to institutionalize desired behaviors is through the power of story. Authors Chip Bell and John Patterson share a great example in their book *Take Their Breath Away*. It is the story of a man who walked into a Lexus dealership and told the salesperson that he was considering trading in his BMW for a new Lexus. "I've heard a lot of people talk about your legendary service, and I'm curious if it's legitimate." The salesperson nodded his head with appreciation, thanked the prospective customer for giving Lexus an opportunity to wow him, and then offered to show him around the lot.

The prospective customer politely declined, saying he had just one question to ask. "I took my car in to the BMW dealership earlier this week for routine maintenance. In the process, they removed the ashtray to clean it but forgot to put it back. When I discovered it was missing, I called the service manager. He sincerely apologized, said they had indeed found the wayward ashtray, and noted they would be happy to hold it in the office for me to pick up at my convenience. Now, how would you have handled this situation?"

The Lexus salesperson replied, "Well, sir, it would not have happened since we have a fifty-four-step checklist that includes replacing the ashtray after cleaning. But if it were to have happened, we would not have waited for you to call us." The BMW owner smiled and left the showroom.

That evening after work, the Lexus salesperson drove to the BMW dealership, picked up the customer's ashtray, and surprised him with it at the front door of his home![14]

All companies would be wise to create a repository of outstanding service anecdotes that employees could rally around as a source of inspiration and as a road map for identifying what exceptional performance looks like in the trenches.

Do for the Few What You Wish You Could Do for the Rest
Chances are, in our efforts to seek assistance from a fellow human being, we have all at some point heard some variation of the following lame excuse: "I'm sorry, but I simply can't help you. If I do it for you, I would have to do it for everyone." To this, I say hogwash! If this sentiment were actually true, nobody would ever help anybody. We are not robots, thank you very much.

We often follow a similar thought pattern when it comes to employee recognition. In a sincere effort to be universally fair and equitable, we make decisions not to recognize anybody because we cannot feasibly recognize everybody. Confused yet?

Let me ask you this. Are there certain employees in your organization who are more valuable than others in terms of performance level and cultural fit? Would the unwanted departure of some team members be more devastating than others? If your answer to these questions is yes, then you must find a way to ensure your top players are being recognized as such (and as we have explored, not just via monetary recognition). Though we might all be equal in God's eyes, chances are we are not equal in terms of our organizational contribution. With this in mind, find creative ways to ensure your recognition efforts and resources are distributed accordingly.

Should We Celebrate the Status Quo?

I am often asked why we should recognize employees for "just doing their job." My response is that we should not...at least not formally. By definition, someone who is "just doing their job" is performing the basic duties outlined in their job description. The appropriate recognition for meeting minimum threshold performance is already being delivered in the form of a paycheck. Now, I am not suggesting that baseline performers should not always be treated with humility and respect. They absolutely should. But to formally recognize all of your corporate athletes with the same "participation" trophy sends a dangerous message to the entire organization.

Remember our earlier discussion on the linkage between accountability and recognition? *Accountability without recognition is demoralizing, and recognition without accountability is hollow.* Formal recognition should always be earned based upon clear accountability measures and not freely given without justification. It must be safeguarded for players who regularly exceed expectations and even more so for those who achieve predefined stretch targets.

Next Steps on the Pathway-to-Purpose Journey

→ **How well does your company recognition system link to organizational purpose, mission, core values, and points of competitive differentiation?** Make a commitment to repurpose or redesign any recognition elements that are misaligned.

→ **To what extent do your managers regularly fail to recognize employee *effort* over employee *talent*?** What are the implications of failing to praise team-member effort?

→ **How can leadership better leverage the three workplace conditions needed for job satisfaction: *complexity, autonomy, and a connection between effort and reward*?** Start by incorporating the three conditions into your talent management process. Ask your leaders to provide numerical rankings for each employee assessed.

→ **Review the section in this Chapter on micro-recognition.** Brainstorm with your leadership team to identify ways to enhance any existing micro-recognition programs or develop one or more new ones.

→ **Discuss how recognition and accountability are "two sides of the same coin."** Why can having one without the other be so problematic?

Chapter 8

CAPTIVATING: ATTRACT EXCEPTIONAL TALENT

I f I were to ask pro football fans to cast their vote for the most remarkable individual player statistic in NFL history, a short list of deserving names would rise to the top. Consider former San Francisco 49ers wide receiver Jerry Rice, the all-time league leader in receptions (1,549), total touchdowns (208), and receiving yards (22,895). Or how about all-time league rushing leader Emmitt Smith, of Dallas Cowboys fame, with 18,355 career rushing yards? Of course, few would leave quarterback Tom Brady out of this discussion, who is currently playing in his twentieth year in the NFL. To date, he has thrown for an all-time-best 86,300 passing yards (or forty-nine miles) and 620 touchdown passes and, most importantly, was the main catalyst for an NFL record *six* Super Bowl victories.

My choice for top statistical honors, however, wouldn't crack most fan's top ten or even top one hundred list. In fact, many casual pro football fans may not have even heard of the player who sits alone atop my list. His name is Joe Thomas. Thomas was a left tackle for the Cleveland Browns, who played in the league from 2007 until his retirement in 2018. Huh? What justification could I possibly have in selecting an offensive lineman who played with little national fanfare for a perennially bottom-feeder team?

Let this absurd fact sink in for a moment…Joe Thomas never missed an offensive play in his first eleven NFL seasons. Think about the immensity of this accomplishment. Not only did he never fail to appear in a single *game*, spanning 175 consecutive contests, he literally never missed one…

single…*play*! For those of you into obscure statistics, that adds up to 10,363 consecutive offensive snaps, without ever coming out of a game—not for injury (despite enduring multiple torn/strained knee ligaments, severe ankle sprains, etc.), not for the occasional equipment malfunction or from physical exhaustion or illness or, heck, just answering the call of nature. [1]

While some degree of good fortune certainly played into Thomas's accomplishing such an amazing feat, few would argue that in today's modern NFL, characterized by concussion protocols, imposed minute/play restrictions, and increased pressure to rest marquee players as an injury avoidance strategy, remaining on the field for every down over an extended time period has become increasingly rare. Yet Thomas actually played in today's modern NFL era and did so at such a high level that he is undoubtedly one of the greatest offensive linemen to ever play the game, having been selected to ten consecutive Pro Bowls. So what made Thomas so committed to his craft and to his team, despite the fact that the Browns never even sniffed the playoffs during his career? And what can we learn from his approach to the game when it comes to our organizational talent acquisition efforts?

Recruit Corporate Athletes

As we discovered in chapter 4, regardless of how good you are, you will never achieve to the level that you could within the context of a larger team. In order to *perform* well, you must first *hire* well. It is a basic principle that holds true for any irresistible company. When it comes to fostering irresistible company cultures, nothing is more important than winning the war for talent.

If you fail to recruit the right *corporate athletes* into your enterprise, both in terms of talent and culture fit, you can rest assured there will be a price to pay. Individual, silo-based contributions will only take a company so far. Sustainable excellence requires a team of like-minded people coming together for a common purpose in order to achieve what they could never conceivably achieve by themselves. Joe Thomas was the type of player any top-flight company should aspire to add to its organizational roster. Let's explore several of Thomas's key character traits that we should be looking for in exemplary job applicants.

Practice Resilience

Resilience is characterized by the ability to recover from setbacks, adapt well to change, and keep going in the face of adversity. Joe Thomas could very well be the poster child for resilience. Consider again the immensity of never missing a single offensive play in eleven seasons. Yet, also realize the environment in which Thomas performed his job. It was not as if the Cleveland Browns were a perennial playoff team, or even a mediocre one, during his illustrious career. In fact, it could be argued that Thomas was the greatest player in league history whose team never reached the playoffs. Even more shocking, the Browns had just one winning season during Thomas's career...his rookie campaign. Here is my point. Thomas had every imaginable excuse to lie down in the face of enduring adversity. Few people could resist the temptation to lower their personal standards on a championship-caliber team, but it is hard to imagine anyone never doing so on a team that consistently lost more than it won. Joe Thomas never relented. He was extraordinarily resilient.

With regard to talent acquisition, are you and your fellow leaders going out of your way to hire people who can successfully manage through adversity? No matter how gifted or accomplished an individual might be, they will become a millstone around the neck of your organization if they mentally/emotionally check out when things get tough. And rest assured, things will get tough at some point. They always do.

Focus on We...Not Me

As we discussed extensively in chapter 4, enduring organizational success is grounded on developing a cohesive group of individuals with a unified resolve and passion to serve. Many enterprises fall prey to the allure of acquiring rainmakers, particularly in their quest to fill critical sales roles. In many instances, these top performers have attained near mythical status based upon their otherworldly history of success with a competing company. They are showered with outrageous bonus and incentive offers by would-be suitors attempting to entice them to greener pastures. This approach sounds fine in theory, but it can often turn out far differently than expected.

Suppose the rainmaker ends up being a prima donna with an inflated view of themselves, who believes everyone else should simply bow to their every whim? Would the increased financial top-line and/or ancillary value resulting from this person's efforts be worth the potential long-term damage inflicted on your company's morale and culture? These are answers you and senior leaders must answer. Regardless, I would urge you to consider your company's collective philosophy on this topic *before* you encounter it in the real world. Now is better than later, and now will make later better.

Irresistible cultures never compromise culture fit for ego-driven stars. Of course, your best-case scenario is to hire the most talented and capable individual performers who will also be among your best team players. Avoiding the allure of a high-performing culture killer is undoubtedly one of our biggest opportunities (and challenges) when it comes to talent acquisition.

We see the chilling effects of a me-versus-we mentality played out in professional sports all the time. Elite athletes are drafted (hired) by organizational talent evaluators who are intoxicated by the individual skill they see on the field while overlooking various red flags suggesting that the candidate is either unwilling or unable to operate effectively within a team context. Though the Cleveland Browns have certainly made more than their share of player personnel blunders over the years, they unquestionably got it right in 2007 when drafting Joe Thomas. NFL quarterback Josh McCown had this to say about his former teammate:

> Playing with Joe Thomas was great because every time you came onto the field, you knew two things were going to happen. Joe was always smiling, and he was going to be at the top of his game. A consummate pro, my favorite memories of Joe are watching him work with young guys, taking a young O-lineman aside and working on the details of playing the position, and not only at tackle, but guard. He saw the big picture, and I think that's what makes him special. He's a great teammate and player, and I am very thankful to have been a teammate of Joe Thomas.[2]

Despite being one of the few individual bright spots on a team that struggled woefully around him, consider that Thomas never once asked to be traded to another organization stocked with superior talent, a stable culture, and a realistic shot at making a deep playoff run. He remained selfless throughout, refusing to waver in his commitment to teammates, organization, and the city of Cleveland.

Just Do Your Job!
Earlier in my career, I made the mistake of hiring someone who I felt certain was the perfect match for an important job opening. To this day, I remain convinced that the individual's skill set and qualifications were the ideal fit to flourish in the role. The problem, as I would soon discover, was that while she was more than capable, my new hire was not really interested in doing what I hired her to do.

After the first few weeks on the job, I noticed the newbie beginning to avoid some of her key responsibilities in favor of ones she deemed more important/appealing. Upon addressing my concerns, the employee shared her desire to "tweak my job duties just a bit to better align with my future career aspirations." It wasn't that she was lazy or maliciously being insubordinate. She just had a different agenda that was incongruent with what we needed her to do.

Now, I am all for hiring people with great ambition and a desire to continuously learn and grow. These are essential attributes to building a successful team. But they are not the only attributes. As part of my due diligence, I failed on a couple of levels during the earlier recruitment phase. First, while the specifications outlined in the job description were sufficient, I should have been clearer from the outset regarding my expectation that they be strictly adhered to. Second, I should have confirmed during the interview process that the candidate fully understood said responsibilities and was in complete agreement to carry them out on a daily basis. While there is no guarantee things would have turned out differently, I would have at least done my part to bring about a more desirable outcome.

It is likely that no one in NFL history ever more effectively excelled at what they were hired to do than Joe Thomas. He consistently played with a level of skill and attention to detail rarely seen in any endeavor. Keep in mind that one of the most critical responsibilities of any offensive lineman is to protect his quarterback during a pass play. According to official NFL statistics, Thomas dropped into pass protection 6,680 times during his career. His defender was credited with sacking the quarterback a mere *thirty* instances…a mind-boggling four-tenths of 1 percent! No one performs their job perfectly, but Joe Thomas came pretty darn close!

Listen to what Thomas had to say about his own Hall of Fame career:

> To be honest, I never set out to do it. It just sort of happened. It's ingrained in you as a young athlete: "Get up! Play the next play!" It's the job. You know, obviously, the losing hurts. I'm human. But something I've found comfort in is, *Just do your job.* I've got people in my family who get up and go to work every day and they don't complain. Regardless of the record, I get to play a kids' game. I am blessed to do what I love to do so much.[3]

Demonstrate Passion and Purpose

I find Joe Thomas's comments above to be incredibly inspiring. They provide great wisdom and insight for leaders and teammates alike. So much of individual and collective success is predicated on the simple mantra of "Just do your job," to perform every seemingly mundane task to the very best of our ability—even when, in isolation, our efforts might seem insignificant. Joe Thomas showed up day after day, year after year, with authentic passion and purpose…"I get to play a kid's game. I am blessed to do what I love to do so much." How many of us would greatly benefit simply by remembering that each day is a gift?

No one becomes exceptional without believing in what they do and knowing that their efforts matter. Thomas *loved* his job, so much so that he didn't view it as work per se but a kid's game. For more than a decade, he played with an uncommon enthusiasm that all of us should seek to emulate in our careers. As talent evaluators, it is incumbent on us to recruit candidates with an intrinsic fire and not just a demonstrated aptitude.

Take a Recruitment Litmus Test

Do you represent the type of company that the job candidates you are looking for are looking for? Would you steer someone you care deeply about to your workplace for a job opportunity? If you were personally looking for a job that would genuinely inspire and challenge you, would you be drawn to your company? Your honest answers to these questions are strong indicators of your organization's current status as an employer of choice. They also speak volumes about the irresistibility of your company culture.

What points of differentiation are you promoting as part of your overall recruitment strategy? The most coveted job seekers want their efforts to matter. They are determined to find meaning in their jobs, not just money in their jobs. Beyond merely turning a profit, they also expect to profit emotionally and psychologically. Following are critical factors to consider as you look to continuously upgrade your company talent.

Evaluate for Cultural Fit

For all the talk about hiring fit, there is still too much emphasis on technical skills and experience when it comes to interviewing and selection. And this happens at all levels. When push comes to shove, most executives get enamored with what candidates know and have done in their careers and allow those things to overshadow more important behavioral issues. They don't seem to buy into the notion that you can teach skill but not attitude.
—Patrick Lencioni, *The Advantage*

In the employee selection process, we must take great care to hire for complementary values. Individual purpose should align with the core beliefs and stated purpose of your organization. Regardless of a candidate's skill set and prior job success, resist the temptation to assume you can turn a potential cultural misfit into a model corporate citizen. You are better off delaying a hire indefinitely to ensure you get the right one than to rush the process and make a huge mistake. It is not unlike the evaluation process many of us follow when considering a potential life partner. It would be foolish to make a long-term marriage commitment based solely on an initial impression. While physical appearance is certainly important, most would agree that getting to know the other person at a heart level is essential. Regardless of how appealing someone might appear to be on the surface, the presence of a common purpose in terms of shared beliefs, religious and political views, and common interests cannot be overestimated. Just as a failed marriage can have dire consequences on the future lives of those involved, so, too, can a poor hire prove to be highly damaging to the culture of an organization.

Despite our very best efforts—despite all the interviews, personality assessments, background checks, reference calls, and drug tests—there will inevitably be situations in which poor cultural fits make their way into our corporate bloodstream. When this occurs, move quickly to "cut your losses" to preserve the integrity of your workplace. Rest assured, your team members will be watching closely to see how you respond to a bad hire.

Fortunately, in most cases your culture (whether positive or toxic) tends to attract similar job seekers. Companies are very much like individuals in this vein. *You attract what you currently are, not what you wish you were or otherwise aspire to be.*

Ensure Managers Play an Active Role

While human resources departments and retained search firms generally play a pivotal role in bringing competent and talented candidates to the forefront, leaders should never expect (or allow) another division or entity to make actual hiring decisions on their behalf. It is simply too important that you get it right, as your professional reputation and the future performance of your team lie in the balance. As it relates to talent selection, the buck ultimately stops with you!

Despite the best intentions of your HR colleagues, only you can properly gauge how well a candidate is likely to fit within the unique cultural undercurrents of your team. Take the necessary time to stay involved throughout the acquisition process, which includes drafting and signing off on the initial job description, receiving regular updates regarding job applicant status, and actively participating during the candidate interviewing phase. Research tells us that it can easily cost a quarter of a million dollars to find and onboard a new employee. Of course, the price tag jumps exponentially if a new hire doesn't actually make it (e.g., recruitment and advertising costs, possible relocation and training expenses, outplacement services, potentially lost customer revenues), not to mention the negative emotional and psychological costs related to managerial stress and team-member morale. It goes without saying that leaders should do everything in their power to make the correct hiring decisions the first time!

Incorporate Candidate Assessment Tools

According to a recent study by the Aberdeen Group, 94 percent of best-in-class organizations use behavioral assessments to support their talent search efforts.[4] That being said, however, assessments should not be used as a stand-alone for hiring decisions. They are designed to be directional in nature, further augmenting other acquisition tools like applicant résumés, education and background checks, reference calls, writing samples, and candidate interviews.

Pre-employment assessments come in many types and flavors, but here are some of the more recognized and scientifically proven tools:

- **Clifton StrengthsFinder.** Unlike many assessment tools that stress candidate weaknesses, StrengthsFinder focuses on applicant proficiencies—the unique talents and abilities individuals bring to their environment. StrengthsFinder themes describe specific patterns of thought, feelings, or behaviors that can be productively applied in a work setting.

- **Predictive Index.** Measures behavioral drives (dominance, extraversion, patience, and formality) as well as cognitive ability. After participants complete the assessment, they are assigned a profile that provides a snapshot of the way they think and work. The data equips leaders to make more informed and objective hiring decisions.

- **Caliper Profile.** Measures an individual's personality characteristics and individual motivations in order to predict on-the-job behaviors and potential. Scientifically validated by nearly six decades of research, the Caliper Profile assessment can be utilized throughout the employee life cycle, including selection.

Look in Nontraditional Places
Today's competitive hiring landscape has never been more uncertain to navigate. In early 2020, unemployment rates in the United States were at a fifty-year low (3.2 percent). Job prospects were in a unique position of strength, with the ability to leverage a market that was desperate for highly experienced and highly skilled candidates. With the onslaught of coronavirus, our economy took a massive hit, and thousands lost their jobs. It is impossible to predict where the job market might stand by the time you read this chapter, but regardless, looking where you have always looked for job candidates will no longer deliver the results you desire. Why? Because the talent acquisition game is not as clear-cut as it used to be. Your talent competitors have become more adept at deploying unconventional recruiting strategies within today's marketplace. If you hope to attract a future wave of exceptional talent, it will require an exceptionally different approach, one that is *strengthened* by ever-changing technology but never *replaced* by it.

For example, contemporary job seeker expects every aspect of their employment search to be easy and efficient. The olden days of browsing the help wanted ads via your local hard copy newspaper are essentially obsolete, but it runs much deeper than digital versus traditional. A growing number of your most qualified applicants are also not content with powering up their laptops or iPads to check out the latest job opportunities. These options lack the convenience and portability for a modern society on the go. In addition, and just as importantly, these choices will not fit in your pocket. Becoming truly relevant to a growing universe of talent requires organizations to ensure their mobile job applicant platform provides an exceptional user experience. Most organizations tend to get it wrong, focusing first on developing the optimal desktop/laptop experience and then settling for a clunky, disjointed mobile solution. Instead, focus first on the smartphone experience, and then build out your desktop experience to match.

No matter how cutting edge your applicant enabled technology is, however, it will never counterbalance the personalized, relational elements necessary to gauge potential talent and organizational fit. Companies like Ritz-Carlton and Chick-fil-A have long been adroit at identifying excellent talent preemptively versus hoping top talent will simply walk through the door or fill out an online application. This "meet you where you are" approach has served both organizations extremely well over the years.

For instance, it is not uncommon for Ritz-Carlton hotel leadership team members to carry a stack of custom business cards with them when off duty to help woo potential top-tier talent. During my tenure with Ritz, I once met a gentleman named Barry Wilson who was working the retail sales floor of an Atlanta area Men's Wearhouse store. Barry's magnetism, extensive product knowledge, and general command of the sales floor were something to behold. When I arrived, Barry was already assisting at least three other customers (maybe more), but his pitch was so genuine and smooth, I felt as if I were his only concern. I entered the store with no real intention of buying anything, but I exited some two hours later with a brand-new wardrobe in tow.

Prior to my encounter with Barry, you would have never caught me spending so much time (or money) shopping for myself in a clothing store. This occasion, however, was uniquely different! After nearly tapping out my credit card, Barry helped me carry everything to my car. I took the opportunity to learn a bit more about him, and I reiterated how impressed I was with his salesmanship. I also told Barry about Ritz-Carlton and our legendary service culture, handed him a business card, and encouraged him to reach out to me directly to discuss potentially joining the company. Though Barry never did take me up on my offer (it turns out he was quite happy and financially secure in his current role), countless other top performers from around the world have been wooed to Ritz-Carlton using similar recruitment best practices.

Recruit with a Relational Approach

Roberta Matuson, a best-selling author, speaker, and consultant in the realm of talent maximization, had this to say about the importance of relational selling in my prior interview with her: "Recruitment has always been and will continue to be a relational business. We must be very wary of relying solely on technology and rekindle the importance of talking with applicants in a conversational way. If you are in a talent recruitment role, you are also 100% in the sales arena." [5]

Matuson's comments are spot on. Just as customers loathe being treated as a meaningless number by the same organizations that relentlessly bombard them with marketing messages, so, too, do candidates long to feel individually valued and connected to the posted job and larger organizational purpose. Instead of feeding your potential talent universe the same tired old sales pitch that the recruitment industry has become synonymous for, be sure to embed your organization's unique points of differentiation into your overall recruiting approach. Be proactive in articulating (verbally and otherwise) why job seekers should be drawn to your company. Talent recruiters have an obligation to promote (i.e., sell) the very best the organization has to offer—with honesty and full disclosure, of course.

Senior leaders at Atlantic Capital Bank (ACB) recently developed a trifold *Purpose Map* designed to internalize the firm's mission to fuel client prosperity, reinforce its core values (creativity, expertise, teamwork, humility, and confidence), and serve as a tangible reminder of organizational success metrics (clients won, clients retained, and client referrals). The purpose maps were so positively received by ACB employees that human resources decided to provide them to external job candidates as well, thereby exposing them early in the recruitment process to the things the bank holds near and dear. In tandem with similar verbiage incorporated into the company's online application site, supplementary recruiting materials, and interview discussion guidelines, the maps help both ACB and applicants better ascertain probable job/organizational alignment and fit. As it relates to job placement, what your company stands for matters. It matters a lot. Make sure each element of your recruiting sales pitch accurately reflects the heart and soul of your organization.

Begin from Within: Employee Referrals

Few things are more critical to a company's client acquisition strategy than developing deep customer relationships. As a key outcome, customers happily refer your products and services to others in their sphere of influence. Customer referrals can and should be the engine that drives your enterprise's growth in the marketplace. As logical as this approach might sound, sales research tells us that actively soliciting existing business referrals is oftentimes one of the last avenues salespeople pursue for new business. While we won't explore the likely reasons for this phenomenon here (this is not a sales book, after all), many companies are missing out on valuable, and likely easier, business opportunities.

In much the same way, extraordinary organizations power their recruitment and talent pipelines by instituting thoughtful and effective *employee* referral strategies. Whether by design or default (hopefully the former), the core values that you and your fellow leaders espouse as the guiding principles of your company are being modeled by a specific group of team members who *get it*, both in terms of their daily output and the greater passion they inspire. These employees embody your organizational true believers.

While we cannot physically replicate our best employees (at least not yet, anyway!), we absolutely have the opportunity to tap into their key circles of influence, and chances are excellent that they are running in the same circles as others who are like-minded. Despite a growing body of evidence indicating employee referrals improve quality-of-hire decisions and retention rates while lowering hiring costs, they remain underutilized in most organizations. According to a study conducted by ERIN, a software company that focuses on human capital management, employee referrals are four times more likely to be hired than non-referrals. Similarly, 82 percent of organizations rate employee referrals above all other sources for generating the best return on investment.[6]

To address this opportunity gap, many organizations have begun formalizing their team-member referral processes. Cloud computing company Digital Ocean launched a new-employee referral incentive structure in early 2017 to help attract top talent. Referring employees receive a $3,500 incentive in addition to a $1,500 charitable donation paid by the company on the team member's behalf. Within twelve months of rollout, 40 percent of the company's new hires had been acquired through referrals.[7]

Google, on the other hand, which reportedly receives more than two million job applications per year, actually began moving away from cash incentives after discovering it was not having the desired impact. It has instead taken a more proactive approach by querying new hires for referrals right away during the onboarding process. Through asking every newbie questions such as "Who is the best salesperson, engineer, marketing manager, etc. you have ever worked for?" and "Who are five to ten people you would want to work with again?" Google soon realized an increase in employee referrals of 33 percent![8] Every organization will need to determine a set of referral strategies that work best for its unique culture. The big idea, though, is that your firm should thoughtfully and deliberately take advantage of the collective talent network of your existing employee base.

Take a Fresh Look at Your Interviewing Approach
The job interview process is a highly inexact discipline. Whether naturally endowed with the ability to wax eloquently or having learned by trial and error how to present themselves in the best possible interview light, certain candidates thrive in an interview setting. Many of us have likely witnessed this firsthand: a promising candidate wows the entire interview panel, the candidate is subsequently hired, and the new employee crashes and burns when it comes time to actually perform. Talk about a frustrating outcome…

The best way to predict how someone will behave (or perform) in the future is to look at how they behaved in the past. Now, don't get me wrong, people can absolutely change over time. This truth is one of the most foundational and critical tenets of the human experience. But unfortunately, substantive behavioral change is most often the exception rather than the rule. It is very hard to do. Fundamental change requires a great deal of self-discipline, and most people, whether consciously or unconsciously, ultimately opt to take the path of least resistance. They stay in their comfort zone, continuing to do what they have always done. As a result, they continue to get what they have always gotten…even if their existing behaviors do not serve them well.

With past behavior generally being a reliable predictor of future behavior, it makes perfect sense to incorporate this type of approach into a structured interview process. The *behavioral interview* is an important tool to assess how prospects previously performed when faced with situations that would be relevant to the new job role. It requires interviewers to ask questions that are more open-ended, and it obliges candidates to share real-world examples from their prior work history.

The *STAR* method is a well-known, behaviorally based interview methodology that has a proven track record of success. Instead of focusing on hypothetical "What *would* you do?" job scenarios, it instead explores tangible, real-life "What *did* you do?" look backs at a candidate's past work experiences. STAR is an acronym for *situation, task, action*, and *result*. Here is a breakdown of how each step works within an interview setting:

Situation. Describe a situation that you were in or a task that you needed to accomplish.
- "Tell me about a time when..."
- "Give me an example of..."

Task. Describe what your responsibility was in that particular scenario.
- "What was your specific task?"
- "What challenges resulted from this situation?"

Action. Explain how you handled the situation or overcame the challenge.
- "What did you do?"
- "How exactly did you handle it?"

Result. Explain the outcome you reached through your actions. If possible, quantify your success or provide concrete examples of the effects of your efforts.
- "What was the result of your actions?"
- "What ended up happening based upon the actions you took?"

As a further enhancement to the STAR methodology, make sure any unique points of organizational differentiation (purpose, mission statement, core values, etc.) are incorporated into your interview questions. This tweak will help you gauge whether the interviewee feedback is congruent with key company principles. For instance, if one of your organizational core values is humility, you might ask an applicant the following question:

"Here at [company name], we believe that having a sense of humility is an important quality in our ability to help our client and fellow team members win. Tell me about a time you demonstrated humility in a prior interaction and how it ultimately played out. What, if anything, did you learn from the situation, and what might you do differently next time?"

Think outside the Traditional Interview Box

I once had a prospective boss invite me to meet him for lunch at a nice restaurant as part of an initial "get to know you" job interview. I thoroughly enjoyed our time together, as it afforded me the chance to both learn more about the job opening and to provide a preliminary pitch on why I believed I was the ideal candidate. So while everything seemed to go well enough, I really didn't give the lunch appointment much more thought. It wasn't until several weeks later, however, after ultimately being hired, that I learned the greater significance of that introductory lunch appointment.

It turns out the hiring manager cleverly leveraged the occasion to evaluate how I would respond to certain scenarios in a seemingly innocuous social setting. For example, when making lunch reservations, he prearranged with restaurant management (in exchange for a promised generous tip) that our assigned server would intentionally mess up my food order! The rationale was that if I was rude and disrespectful to a member of the wait staff, I would likely do the same when interacting with colleagues in a highly charged work situation. In addition, the manager closely observed my general demeanor with regard to looking restaurant personnel in the eye, thanking them for their ongoing service efforts, and demonstrating common decorum for other restaurant patrons. Fortunately, and unbeknownst to me at the time, I "passed" the lunch interview that day with flying colors, and it set the stage for an eventual job offer!

My former manager's creative discovery strategy was an excellent way for us to "peel back the onion" on the true mindset and attitudes of our job applicants, going beyond the sanitized and rote dialogue that is so often the norm with traditional interview approaches.

Of course, there are a variety of other innovative ways to spice up your employee interview process. Some organizations require applicants to complete a designated project or assignment relevant to the job at hand and to subsequently share as part of a follow-up panel interview. Other smart companies ask candidates to develop and deliver formal presentations highlighting why they feel they should be hired for the position. I have even seen scenarios where seriously considered candidates were invited to fine-tune the original organizational job description to better reflect their personal vision for the role and how they believe their unique experience and skills were best suited to successfully deliver on it.

Finally, keep in mind that when it comes to talent acquisition, you are not just hiring an individual but their entire family as well. The general health and well-being of a candidate's personal relationships (particularly familial ones) are often a good indicator of what could be generally expected in the professional realm. There are exceptions, of course, but it is an interpersonal dynamic that should not be overlooked. When applicable and at the appropriate time, consider inviting top candidates to include their spouse or significant other in the interview conversation. You may be surprised what you learn (good or bad)!

Be Respectful to Those Who Don't Make the Cut
Be thoughtful that the culture you espouse shines through even when you have to reject a job candidate. Much earlier in my career, I applied for what I considered a plum position with a well-known organization in the healthcare industry. Following a series of interviews, assessments, and preliminary compensation discussions that took place over the course of several weeks, I felt confident that a job offer was imminent.

I was told by a senior human resources leader that I should expect to hear from the hiring manager within the next week. The next week came and went, and I received no word from anyone; so I reached out to the manager to politely inquire, yet still no response. A second week went by, followed by another and yet another but still no word from anyone. Despite several more attempts to determine my fate, it eventually became clear that the position (and, by extension, the company) that I had once been so enamored with would not be part of my future career plans. My emotions evolved over time from initial confusion to a brief period of disappointment, followed by a tinge of shame and finally cynicism and anger.

Regardless of the company's reasoning for not hiring me, which may have been well founded, it failed to realize in my case (and I suspect others) that its actions highly contradicted the type of reputation it had worked so hard to engender within the marketplace. My perceptions of the organization drastically changed, and one individual's perceptions can play a significant role in either enhancing or diminishing an institution's overall brand image.

Take great care to treat those who don't make the cut with respect and common decency. Think of them in the same way you think of your employees and customers. It is both the right and smart thing to do.

Go Beyond Standard Benefit Offerings

Though I won't spend a lot of time here discussing traditional employer benefits, it is essential that your company offer a competitive set of health care, wellness, paid time off, and retirement offerings. Calling back to Herzberg's motivator-hygiene theory in chapter 7, adequate benefit packages (just like employee compensation) are a prerequisite to get you into the talent game, but they will rarely by themselves compel candidates to choose you over your talent-hungry competitors. But what if we take our benefits game up a notch? Competitive differentiation occurs when your benefits go beyond standard fare and into a more forward-thinking and innovative realm. And by the way, I am not just talking about the addition of Ping-Pong tables and fancy espresso machines.

An organization's commitment to investing in the prosperity and development of their people is among the most attractive forms of benefit offerings. Let's look at a couple of specific examples:

Publix Super Markets
Based in Lakeland, Florida, Publix generated a reported $36.1 billion in revenues in 2018, and at last count was the eighth-largest private company in the country. Founded in 1930 by George W. Jenkins, the supermarket chain is approaching 1,250 stores across seven southeastern states. Publix has been named one of *Fortune*'s 100 Best Companies to Work For an amazing twenty-three consecutive years, finishing at number twelve in 2019.

How has Publix created such an irresistible workplace? There are numerous reasons, but one stands above all the others. You see, with more than two hundred thousand employees, Publix is the largest *employee-owned* company in the world, and it is not even a close race. All workers, regardless of their position in the company, receive on average 10 percent of their annual salary (at no cost to them) in the form of company stock after having been with the company for more than twelve months and put in more than one thousand hours of work.

They are more than just employees. They are co-owners. It is not unusual for a seasoned Publix employee to have accrued more than $1 million through the company's stock program. Though employee stock options obviously won't be a feasible strategy for all organizations, the overall sentiment of treating your employees like owners from an empowerment and personal development perspective can be a real game changer.

In addition to offering an ownership stake to every team member, Publix provides a series of other popular employee benefits, such as the availability of a formal company mentoring program, a structured, on-the-job training curriculum facilitated by departmental experts, and full access to a library of books, videos, and online resources. It is not surprising that Publix commands some of the best and most committed talent in the marketplace. Want further proof that associates are highly engaged? Voluntary turnover rates at Publix are consistently around 5 percent compared to nearly 65 percent for the overall retail industry![9]

Zappos
If you happen to be a shoe aficionado, chances are you are familiar with Seattle-based online retailer Zappos.com. Founded in 1999, Zappos has

experienced explosive growth over recent years, expanding its product lines to include clothing, handbags, and accessories. Annual sales have reached nearly $1 billion. At Zappos, new hires are given the option to take a month's salary in exchange for walking away at around the halfway mark of the intensive four-week training program. The policy is officially called the *Graceful Leave Policy,* but within the Zappos organization, it's commonly referred to as "The Offer." Despite the generous incentive opportunity, more than 97 percent of Zappos's new hires decline the money and stay, which is a powerful indicator of team-member engagement and cultural fit.

Innovative, value-added benefits at Zappos extend well beyond "The Offer."[10] For instance, team members hoping to learn about another department can request to take part in a *shadow session,* whereby they are granted time to observe and collaborate with one or more colleagues in their daily work environment. Depending on the specific employee scenario, shadow sessions can be positioned as a one-time learning event, or they can take place over an expanded time period.

Zappos also employs a team of life coaches whose purpose is to "partner with employees to uncover the path to the best version of themselves." Another offered benefit of note that is still relatively uncommon across corporate America is paid paternity leave. New Zapponian fathers can take up to six weeks of leave that can be used at one time or split into two segments.[11]

Include Additional Benefit Differentiators

Beyond the items covered above, there are a host of other employer benefits that can help differentiate you in the talent marketplace. I will touch on several of them here.

- **Tuition reimbursement.** If you do not currently provide some sort of financial reimbursement for employees seeking to further their education, you could very well be losing out on high quality job candidates, particularly within the millennial and Generation Z populations.

- **Employee emergency fund.** These programs are generally established by a given organization and funded by employees who voluntarily donate a portion of their earnings to assist fellow colleagues hit by unexpected financial hardships (medical treatments, burial costs, natural catastrophe expenses, etc.).

- **Corporate chaplaincy.** Chaplaincy programs are designed to help team members bring their whole self to the workplace: physical, emotional, and spiritual. Services generally include regularly scheduled worksite visits from dedicated chaplains, which are totally voluntary for interested employees, as well as off-site chaplain visits conducted upon employee request. Well-known chaplaincy provider organizations include Corporate Chaplains of America and Marketplace Chaplains.

- **Corporate wellness offerings.** Benefits in the corporate wellness realm have exploded in the workplace of late. Make sure your organization is up to speed on specific offerings like stress reduction, weight loss, smoking cessation, and exercise programs, as well as health risk assessments, health screenings, and nutrition education.

- **Leadership development.** The most irresistible organizations on the planet understand that their long-term success hinges on the continuous growth and development of their leaders. Much more on this topic in the next chapter, but for now let me just say that the significance of nurturing a resilient leadership base cannot be overstated.

Next Steps on the Pathway-to-Purpose Journey

→ **What are your impressions of the STAR approach to interviewing?** Consider tasking your HR team with developing a formal template for conducting interviews. Formulate a strategy for deploying the template to applicable managers who will be involved in conducting candidate interviews in the future.

→ **How would you assess the overall effectiveness of your current recruitment process?** Collaborate with your senior leadership team to identify two to three key actions you will take to enhance recruitment efforts based upon content drawn from this chapter.

→ **What is your company's current communication process for job candidates who don't make the cut?** What steps will you take to ensure these individuals are treated with honor and respect?

→ **Does your organization currently use any standardized assessments to help with the talent selection process?** If yes, how would you rate the effectiveness of the tool(s)? If not, consider whether incorporating one or more tools might be beneficial.

→ **Work with your human resources team to itemize and record all employee benefit offerings.** Evaluate whether your standard benefits package is robust enough to ensure you are consistently winning when it comes to talent acquisition. Consider the potential ramifications of any missing benefit elements for both existing employees and desired future ones.

Chapter 9

SUSTAINING: PRESERVE THE IRRESISTIBLE

In chapter 8, we explored best practices for acquiring top-shelf talent. Whether in the realm of big-time sports or in the context of the corporate boardroom, the job of talent evaluators is never finished. We must constantly assess our organizational talent landscape, preemptively seeking opportunities to upgrade overall team performance and employee engagement levels. Shrinking profit margins, external competitive pressures, and unexpected environmental shifts can inevitably force our hand in making difficult "roster" changes. At times, certain team members may be required to take on modified job roles, while others may be terminated due to underperformance or behavioral issues. Of course, in a free market system, employees hold certain powers as well, including the right to further their career elsewhere.

The key point here is that acquisition is only half of the organizational talent equation. Once we have identified and secured whom we believe to be the most qualified candidate for a given position, it becomes incumbent on the enterprise as a whole to keep them around, to best position them for immediate and long-term success. Too many organizations invest tremendous time and expense on the front end procuring new talent, only to "throw them into the fire" once they are brought on board. This approach, of course, is a big mistake. Think of it like an NFL team that drafts a highly promising player but fails to provide him with a playbook or any form of individualized coaching. Both the player and the organization are sure to suffer.

In this final chapter, we will review key strategies for maximizing the talent residing inside your workforce, from the early stages of new-hire orientation and onboarding to longer-term priorities like leadership development and performance evaluations.

Make the First Impression Count

You are no doubt familiar with the well-worn cliché "You never get a second chance at a first impression." Nowhere is this truer than with someone starting a new job. Leading up to the point of new hire, chances are good that all involved from within have collectively put their best foot forward. New hires have likely been presented with a narrative that depicts the organization in its best possible light, a narrative characterized by welcoming and collaborative teammates, outstanding career development potential, and an overall great place to work. This recruitment pitch is rarely intended to be deceptive or misleading; it simply skews more toward the ideal and the aspirational.

In *The Power of Moments*, a *New York Times* best-selling book, authors Chip Heath and Dan Heath explore how certain defining occasions in the human experience tend to have an extraordinary impact on our lives: an encouraging teacher who first complimented you on your vocal ability, thus arming you with the needed courage to launch a highly successful singing career; a chance encounter with a stranger who would ultimately become your best friend and forever soul mate; an early morning house call from police officers informing you that an armed burglar shot and severely injured your teenage son.

The Heath brothers note that while many human experiences are the result of fate or chance, we have an opportunity as human beings to personally shape life's most meaningful and memorable moments. They go on to point out that a new hire's first day on the job is one worthy of considerable organizational focus and investment. This defining event represents three major transitions for the incoming employee: *intellectual* (new work), *social* (new people), and *environmental* (new place).

Consider the day one employee experience designed by John Deere, an iconic manufacturer of agricultural, construction, and forest machinery. The program was initially deployed by the company for its Asia-based markets. Here is a narrative example provided by the Heath brothers detailing a first day at Deere:

> Shortly after you accept the offer letter from John Deere, you get an email from a John Deere Friend. Let's call her Anika. She introduces herself and shares some of the basics: where to park, what the dress norms are, and so forth. She also tells you that she'll be waiting to greet you in the lobby at 9 a.m. on your first day.
>
> When your first day comes, you park in the right place and make your way to the lobby, and there's Anika! You recognize her from her photo. She points to the flatscreen monitor in the lobby—it features a giant headline: "Welcome, Arjun!"
>
> Anika shows you to your cubicle. There's a six-foot-tall banner set up next to it—it rises above the cubes to alert people that there's a new hire. People stop by over the course of the day to say hello to you.
>
> As you get settled, you notice the background image on your monitor: It's a gorgeous shot of John Deere equipment on a farm at sunset, and the copy says, "Welcome to the most important work you'll ever do."
>
> You notice you've already received your first email. It's from Sam Allen, the CEO of John Deere. In a short video, he talks a little bit about the company's mission: "to provide the food, shelter, and infrastructure that will be needed by the world's growing population." He closes by saying, "Enjoy the rest of your first day, and I hope you'll enjoy a long, successful, fulfilling career as part of the John Deere team."

Now you notice there's a gift on your desk. It's a stainless steel replica of John Deere's original "self-polishing plow," created in 1837. An accompanying card explains why farmers loved it.

At midday, Anika collects you for a lunch off-site with a small group. They ask about your background and tell you about some of the projects they're working on. Later in the day, the department manager (your boss's boss) comes over and makes plans to have lunch with you the next week.

You leave the office that day thinking, I belong here. The work we're doing matters. I matter to them.[1]

John Deere's day one program in Asia created such fanfare that domestic employees began asking (tongue and cheek) if they could "quit and be hired again"! It should be noted that with a little resourcefulness and ingenuity, organizational approaches like the one developed for John Deere can be repurposed for companies operating in a highly virtual onboarding environment. A growing number of forward-thinking organizations have leveraged emerging technologies such as Microsoft Teams and Zoom to help successfully navigate remote onboarding in the COVID-19 era.

Here are several essentials that every organization should integrate into the newcomer experience.

- **Communicate early and often.** Designate a team member (preferably an enthusiastic and outgoing one) to serve as a communication liaison with all new hires prior to their start date. Have the team member reach out well in advance via videoconference to make initial introductions and cover specific instructions regarding what to expect on the first day (office driving directions, detailed parking information, security/clearance guidelines, proper attire, whom to contact upon arrival, etc.). Ensure cell phone numbers are exchanged in case there are any last-minute changes or questions.

- **Design a warm welcome.** Organizations should go out of their way to ensure new hires receive a memorable welcome on their first day. Do not just assume this will occur spontaneously, as it rarely pans out that way. Instead, thoughtfully plan a high impact greeting into your day one onboarding strategy. Memorable elements may include highlighting new-hire names via digital monitors in the lobby or office areas (see the Deere story above), decorating new hire offices/workstations with creative signage and streamers, or hosting a breakfast with pertinent supervisors and company executives delivering some poignant, introductory remarks.

- **Leverage technology.** Many of us have endured the frustration of arriving to a new job filled with great excitement and anticipation, only to discover our laptop, desk phone, and/or company-issued cellphone have not been properly set up. Talk about a bad first impression! Make sure your technology folks are on point to prevent this from totally undermining the intended newcomer experience. It is a common problem that can *always* be avoided with proper planning and execution.

- **Provide proper structure.** Undertaking any significant challenge in our lives, like starting a new job, can be very exciting, but it can also be highly stressful in nature—particularly if there is a lack of initial certainty and structure. With this in mind, new hires should be given a clearly outlined agenda for day one, at a minimum. Many great places to work actually provide structured itineraries covering multiple weeks. Being surrounded by new faces in a totally new environment, with a new set of performance expectations, is daunting enough. But facing all this newness with limited guidance and direction can be overwhelming. Equip new hires with a road map to help fuel their success and engagement from the very beginning!

Start Strong: New-Hire Orientation

A great orientation program is the most powerful resource at our disposal for successfully welcoming and integrating new team members into the corporate tribe. It is the foundational bedrock to ensure the newest members of our corporate family understand and embrace what the organization stands for and how it makes a difference in the lives of your key stakeholders. Simply put, new-hire orientation is a pathway to purpose that lays the early groundwork for irresistible cultures. In fact, research compiled by Click Boarding, an onboarding software company, revealed that new employees who attend a well-structured orientation program are 69 percent more likely to remain at their company for up to three years.[2]

As a quick point of clarification, the terms *orientation* and *onboarding* are not the same. Onboarding refers to a series of events/activities that normally take place over the first sixty to ninety days of employment. The primary purpose of onboarding is to help newcomers become acclimated and competent at performing the day-to-day mechanics of their jobs. On the whole, onboarding is generally geared more toward educating the head than it is nourishing the heart. It is more left-brain oriented (logical and intuitive).

In contrast, orientation is a single event designed to welcome new hires into the organization and begin the process of cultural immersion. Orientation tends to be much more right-brain oriented (emotional and expressive). In consulting with numerous companies over the years, I've heard some variation of the following sentiment numerous times: "We already have an excellent onboarding process, so there is really no need to pull our new hires away from their jobs and force them to sit through an orientation program." I highly caution against this mentality, as again, new-hire orientation, when executed properly, is highly inspirational and experiential. It sets the emotional tone and tenor for the overarching employee experience. New-hire orientation should be treated as a non-negotiable and deeply transformational cultural imperative.

Let's spend some time now exploring some additional ingredients essential to serving up an exceptional orientation event.

Embrace the Primacy of Immediacy

Shepherding your new hires through a formal orientation event should never be delayed beyond their first few days on the job. The faster that employees become immersed in the essential elements of your culture, the better they will be positioned to fuel company prosperity and to experience greater personal purpose. This dynamic of immediacy reminds me of the process some families undergo in order to adopt a child. No benevolent parents would go through the extensive rigors of adoption and, upon finally gaining custody, fail to lovingly welcome their newest family member into the home while also expressing their unwavering commitment to the child's well-being and ongoing development. Neither would the parents delay sharing the key values and beliefs that serve as cultural guideposts for how they treat each other internally and those outside the family dynamic.

In much the same way, delaying new-hire orientation tends to mute its intended impact. Newbies are likely to begin forming their own assumptions regarding what the organization holds as sacred and true. Similarly, it may signal that orientation is simply not something the institution holds in high regard, serving as more of a checklist requirement than a foundational cornerstone of your culture.

Now granted, the logistics of scheduling recurring orientation events, particularly for companies with irregular hiring patterns, can be quite challenging. But the most employee-centric organizations develop processes to ensure *all* new hires go through orientation right away. At Ritz-Carlton, for example, new-employee orientation is scheduled twice per month (generally every other Monday). Newbies may not start in their roles without first attending their hotel's immersive two-day orientation program. Hiring managers know there are no exceptions to this rule, so they must plan accordingly with this cadence in mind. Ritz-Carlton understands that employees will not truly feel a part of the organization unless they are exposed to its expectations and values from the outset.

Include Executive Presence

Another extremely important element of highly effective orientation programs is senior leadership involvement. Unlike so many companies that rely solely on frontline HR or training personnel to establish the proper climate with new hires, exceptional ones like Atlantic Capital Bank (ACB), first introduced in chapter 2, do things a bit differently. A two-time *Atlanta Business Chronicle* Best Place to Work and *American Banker* Best Banks to Work For recipient, ACB's orientation program, *ExperienceACB!,* is almost exclusively facilitated by the bank's executive leadership team.

The CEO kicks off the two-day event with an in-depth summary of the organization's distinctive history and culture. Interspersed between an elaborate scavenger hunt, guided tour of corporate headquarters, and multiple employee meet and greets, the other executive team members also spend dedicated time sharing and interacting during orientation. Each leader provides a thorough overview of their division and goes on to describe how all teams work cross-functionally to help fulfill the bank's purpose and vision.

Provide Historical Context

Every organization has an origin story—a distinctive narrative that birthed it into existence. Communicating your origin story helps foster a sense of corporate belonging and pride, unifying your people around a common, historical context that is unlike any other on the planet. Make sure to widely communicate and celebrate this story, particularly with new hires.

The beginnings of software giant Microsoft in the childhood garage of co-founder Bill Gates is a legendary origin story. Or consider Matt Maloney and Mike Evans, two nondescript software developers from Chicago who grew increasingly frustrated calling local restaurants in search of takeout food. Their solution to the problem? In 2004, Maloney and Evans rolled out a fledgling restaurant-food delivery company called Grubhub, which is currently valued at $6.7 billion! Just as every individual has a unique backstory, so, too, does every enterprise.[3]

The term *cultural artifact* has become very popularized in the business arena over the past several years. Cultural artifacts are objects or concepts that supplement the larger organizational narrative, further codifying corporate values and points of competitive differentiation. Some company artifacts, like the Ritz-Carlton *Credo Card* referenced in chapter 3, are tangible. Others, like the famous Nike "swoosh" logo, may be less concrete, but they are equally important for injecting the company storyline into the hearts and minds of new employees.

Define Conditions of Satisfaction

Imbue newcomers with clear expectations for mutual success. The orientation process should cover designated behaviors deemed by the organization to be essential for individual and corporate success. These behaviors are most often articulated in the form of cultural imperatives, such as organizational purpose/mission, vision, and core values. By the same token, conditions of satisfaction should also be established and communicated in terms of what new team members should expect from their employer. For instance, technology giant Cisco, which in 2020 finished at the very top of the *Fortune* Best Places to Work list, outlines its commitment to team members as part of a manifesto called "The People Deal" (reference figure 9.1).

What you can expect from us:

We'll help connect you with the people, information and opportunities you need to succeed. And we'll set the direction to meet our customers' needs, with the speed required in today's market, and change the world for the better.

We'll provide an open and agile environment to explore your best ideas, challenge the norm, and develop your skills to help us disrupt the market and lead the way to a better tomorrow.

We'll welcome you to a team of the best and brightest; where your development is supported and we recognize the value of your contribution. Our satisfaction comes from our collective ability to make a meaningful difference in the world.

Cisco Systems People Deal - Figure 9.1

Incorporate Interactive and Gamification Elements

Today's employees are not content with conventional new-hire orientation methodologies, replete with one-sided monologues and reams of disparate facts and figures. Generations Y and Z, in particular, expect more than just talking heads and tired PowerPoint slides. They want to be entertained and inspired at the same time they learn. Consider using quickly evolving mobile apps like Kahoot! or OrgLynx to deliver interactive spice and modern gamification elements to your orientation program. Video and musical/audio features can also be highly impactful. Even largely old-school activities like icebreakers, team-based skits, game show simulations, and team-building exercises can help set the stage for a highly memorable and immersive orientation experience.

Beware of Excessive Paperwork

I don't know anyone who enjoys filling out paperwork. Clearly, form filling is a necessary reality in our modern work environment from both a legal and compliance point of view, but there are ways to minimize its pervasiveness in the orientation arena. For instance, many companies are successfully harnessing the power of popular human resources information system (HRIS) software programs such as UKG Pro, Paycom, and Workday to help navigate the new-employee paperwork dilemma. In many cases, a variety of forms, acknowledgments, and documentation can be efficiently completed by newcomers prior to their first day on the job.

Seek Continuous Feedback

As with any major initiative or event, collecting feedback from key stakeholders is a must. It is no different when it comes to assessing the effectiveness of new-hire orientation. Make it easy and psychologically safe for newcomers to express their unvarnished opinions by inviting them to participate in a confidential post-orientation survey or third-party facilitated interview.

While it is important to keep any feedback process as brief as possible to avoid participant fatigue, don't sacrifice obtaining input that supplies actionable improvement insights. For example, if multiple respondents note dissatisfaction with the marketing presentation delivered during orientation, it would be important that the solicited feedback include an opportunity for respondents to provide additional clarity: Were concerns due to the marketing content covered, presentation handouts, facilitator effectiveness, or something else? Greater specificity will allow organizers to make more informed program enhancements going forward.

Hardwire Future Success into Employee Onboarding Tactics

As mentioned earlier, employee onboarding encompasses a set of structured activities that occur during the initial stages of a new hire's employment. Just like new-hire orientation, taking shortcuts with the onboarding process is highly discouraged. Research (and common sense) reveals that extended onboarding time frames has numerous benefits, including higher employee retention, improved worker productivity, enhanced levels of mutual trust (psychological safety), greater team-member collaboration, and faster times to peak productivity.

Despite the proven advantages of longer onboarding periods, it appears that most organizations have chosen to ignore the data. According to research conducted by CareerBuilder, nearly three-quarters of human resources professionals say that their current onboarding process lasts one month or less, while almost 50 percent of respondents note that onboarding lasts a week or less. Only one in ten has an onboarding program that extends to three months or more.[5]

So, what is the ideal time span for an exceptional new-hire onboarding experience? While no magic number has been identified to date, best-in-class organizations tend to fall somewhere in the sixty-to-one-hundred-day range. Of course, no onboarding program, regardless of how lengthy it might be, will have a marked impact in the absence of certain key elements, four of which are highlighted as follows.

Implement a Buddy System

Starting as early as day one, pair up new hires with a designated peer. These "peer buddies" should be well-respected, high-performing employees, with no direct supervising authority over the onboarding employee. In this critical role, buddies are charged with helping colleagues navigate their new environment. They are happy to share their firsthand experiences with new colleagues and answer any questions or concerns that may surface along the way. For instance, peer buddies may coordinate introductions with key internal stakeholders, educate newbies on information related to potential political land mines, or simply point out local hot spots for lunch.

It should be noted that the peer buddy process is not intended as a replacement for a traditional mentor, who is typically more experienced and involved in the all-around development of an employee. More to come on mentorship programs later.

Emphasize Relational Onboarding

Design your onboarding process to connect with employees at both a head and heart level. Treat onboarding as a relationship-building opportunity, not just a list of humdrum transactional activities. An extended onboarding process that incorporates both structured and unstructured dialogue allows for more in-depth, personalized interactions and greater collaborative learning across the enterprise. While mastering the fundamentals of one's job is a necessary and worthy pursuit, so, too is forging lasting emotional connections with fellow colleagues.

Remember...*logic makes you think, but emotion makes you act.* We are by nature emotional beings, and irresistible cultures (and the individuals who make them up) flourish in environments characterized by mutually beneficial and purpose-driven relationships.

Quantify and Build on Team Member Strengths

In chapter 8, we discussed pre-hire assessment tools like StrengthsFinder and Talent Plus, which provide directional insights during the acquisition process. These tools can also be successfully leveraged post-hire to better steer team members toward their strengths and to increase their awareness of potential blind spots. Take me, for instance. My most dominant talent theme, as identified from my responses to StrengthsFinder, is achiever. As the name implies, achiever explains my continuous drive for accomplishment. It is a talent theme that has served me quite well in the past, but left unchecked, achiever can also become a major thorn in my side. It turns out that I have the tendency to project my achievement drive onto others in the form of unrealistic expectation and demands—not a character trait that will exactly inspire others to trust my guidance or want to follow me!

The good news in all of this for my development is that a former manager once sat me down, educated me on my assessment results, and coached me on how to take advantage of my strengths while also preventing them from becoming liabilities. As leaders, we would be wise to do the same for our team members.

Establish Early Wins
As we have noted already, the initial stages of a new job can be daunting. The immense learning curve required to reach a personal state of homeostasis can make even the most confident and competent new hires question their recent career decision. During this critical juncture, leaders should work closely with their employees to establish a series of success milestones, or "early wins." These early wins could take many forms—completing all required compliance training within the first two weeks of employment, meeting personally with each division head by day thirty, establishing regular one-on-ones with subordinates by day forty-five, partnering with a seasoned counterpart to finish an important but realistic project by day sixty, etc. Establishing early, winnable milestones will equip your employees with the confidence they need in the moment while setting the stage for lasting success.

Continuous Talent Management
Garry Ridge, the wildly successful CEO of the WD-40 Company, whom I first introduced in chapter 4, is a self-proclaimed, "learning-obsessed maniac." In fact, all of Ridge's six-hundred-plus employees are required to take what is affectionately referred to as the WD-40 *Maniac Pledge*. As you will see below, the pledge speaks directly to the company's relentless obsession with accountability and learning.

At WD-40, continuous learning is a fully synergistic endeavor, with responsibility shared by both employee and enterprise. To accentuate his personal commitment to the WD-40 learning philosophy, Ridge includes the phrase *ancora imparo* in the signature line of every email communication.

These Italian words mean "I am still learning." Similarly, Ridge is quick to point out the importance of being freed up to learn from our shortcomings without a sense of personal shame or fear of company reprisal. "We don't look at mistakes as mistakes at WD-40," says Ridge. "They are always referred to as learning moments."[6]

So, what key insights can we glean from Garry Ridge about learning? More than anything, it is embracing a philosophy of learning as an unrelenting, never-ending quest. The unfortunate reality, however, is that most people (and most organizations) either don't share this viewpoint, or they fail to actively live it out.

On a personal note, if you believe that becoming an avid reader is an essential pathway to learning, you will both chuckle and cringe at the following joke.

A bookseller conducting a market survey asked a woman, "Which book has helped you most in your life?"

The woman replied, "My husband's checkbook!"

Over the final pages of this chapter, we will explore several practical strategies and concepts to help fully develop the emergent talents of your workforce. Assimilating these strategies into your talent development model will bolster your status as an employer of choice and fuel an organizational culture that team members will find irresistible.

Prioritize Leadership Development

As underscored throughout this book, the long-standing success of any organization ultimately hangs on the continued development of its leadership base. Even the most growth-minded and aspirational leaders need help reaching their full potential and becoming men and women of influence.

Some larger institutions have taken a grassroots approach to leadership development by creating their own academies or centers of excellence. Professionals from a range of disciplines, including curriculum design, learning theory, behavioral modification, and facilitation techniques are carefully selected to manage the effort from within. More resource-constrained organizations tackle the leader growth challenge through some combination of external consultants, industry trade association programs, local college/

university alliances, and online learning subscription platforms. Regardless of your organizational stance, it would be wise to incorporate the following best practices into your leader development toolbox:

- **Embrace blended learning tactics.** Chances are that individuals entering the program will be at varying points on their leadership journey, and they will bring to bear very diverse backgrounds and preferred learning styles. Taking each of these factors into account, be thoughtful to design a strategy with a range of instructional methodologies to include traditional and virtual classroom delivery, online learning capabilities, role-play simulations, problem-solving exercises, training videos, reading assignments, and group project work.

- **Properly balance theory and application.** Training professionals tend to spend way too much time teaching leadership theory and too little time demonstrating practical application. Both are obviously essential. Theory helps us ascertain the *what* and *why* behind our actions, while application speaks to the *how*, or the process of actually *doing something* with the knowledge learned. When addressing program curriculum and delivery, make sure participants always walk away with relevant knowledge they can immediately begin putting into practice. Remember, just because your content is interesting, or even inspiring, does not make it applicable in a real-world setting!

- **Prioritize interpersonal skills.** In his best-selling book *What Got You Here Won't Get You There*, Marshall Goldsmith explains that as leaders move up the ladder in their professional careers, enduring success gradually becomes less about technical expertise and more about addressing interpersonal skill gaps. "At the higher levels of organizational life, all the leading players are technically skilled... The candidate with superb people skills will win out every time."[7] There is a strong tendency in leadership development circles to view the mastery of "soft" skills like active listening, effective coaching, and trust building as somehow less important than learning to read a balance sheet or putting together a compelling sales proposal. This is a dangerous mindset to endorse as we seek to grow our leaders. Proficiency in technical matters is pretty much a given at senior management levels. But the same cannot be said for interpersonal skills. Think about it...every leader will eventually hit a career ceiling if they are unable to get along with other people.

- **Continuously seek participant input.** As with any training endeavor, regular participant feedback is key. I recommend soliciting both in-process and postmortem feedback as part of every development event, regardless of how well you feel a particular session may have gone. Work diligently to cultivate a trusted environment where leaders embrace the value of both giving and receiving constructive criticism. While some degree of structure is important, stay nimble enough to pivot when necessary based upon participant input and body language. I learned this firsthand years ago when directing an external team of young managers through a twelve-month leadership development program. Within thirty minutes of kicking off a particular workshop—one for which I had spent an inordinate amount of time preparing—it became rather obvious that my carefully coordinated message was failing to hit the mark. After probing a bit, the team shared with me that a beloved colleague had unexpectedly passed away in her sleep the prior evening. The group was understandably devastated and uncertain how to best help their teammates through such an emotional valley. Needless to say, at this point I called an audible and proceeded to throw my carefully planned lesson out the window. Instead, we spent our remaining time together that day engaged in productive dialogue around how to lead well in periods of significant pain and disruption.

Establish Mentorship Programming

While I could easily dedicate a full chapter or even entire book to the topic of mentorship, for now I will share some key overarching thoughts and suggestions. I have been very fortunate to participate in formal mentor and mentee capacities, and I can readily attribute much of my professional success to the power of these relationships. A well-designed mentorship program should be an essential part of your talent management strategy. Not convinced? Research tells us that 71 percent of Fortune 500 companies have mentoring programs. [8] In addition, we know that mentees are promoted five times more often than those without mentors, and mentors are six times more likely to be promoted. [9] Lastly, 67 percent of businesses report an increase in productivity due to mentoring relationships.[10]

Whether you are constructing a corporate mentorship program from scratch or evaluating opportunities to improve an existing one, consider these five mentorship essentials:

1. Not all employees will share the same level of passion for a mentor or mentee role. Keeping this factor in mind, promote program participation as an *optional* developmental benefit. This approach will help narrow your candidate pool to those with a genuine interest in the process; plus, you will quickly learn who is serious about personal development and/or contributing to the growth of others.

2. Use a highly structured and coordinated approach when pairing mentors with mentees. It will be important that participant personalities are carefully considered for compatibility. Similarly, be certain that what the mentee seeks to achieve through the program aligns with the specific skill set and expertise a potential mentor would bring to the table.

3. Craft a set of guiding principles that support mentors in leading the mentorship relationship. Train mentors on how to facilitate sessions to ensure maximum effectiveness. Work to institute a standardized approach that does not constrain mentor autonomy.

4. Design a mentor-mentee contract template to be filled out independently prior to program launch and then finalized collaboratively during the first session. The mentor-mentee contract should cover program specifics, including meeting frequency, program objectives, key deliverables, and a statement of partner confidentiality.

5. Provide a centralized tool for mentors to note key milestones and record ongoing mentee progress throughout the partnership period. Some common HRIS systems now have the functionality to design such a tool. Otherwise, a well-designed Excel spreadsheet will likely do the trick.

Reimagine Performance Reviews

Susie was delighted (not really) that her company's annual performance review period had finally arrived. After all, this would likely be her one opportunity over the next twelve months to formally sit down with her boss and learn how he really perceived her work efforts. The thought of hearing her manager subjectively opine about her performance relative to a set of obscure objectives that had long ago lost their relevance was extremely exciting to Susie. After all, who doesn't thoroughly enjoy a pivotal conversation that plays out like Forrest Gump's famous declaration "Life is like a box of chocolates…You never know what you're going to get!"? And in the case of Susie, the ramifications of this single meeting held critical importance for her immediate career trajectory and financial standing.

Of course, Susie's rosy disposition in anticipation of her pending performance appraisal is absurd. I have yet to meet an employee worth their salt who could care less about how their performance is being assessed. And not just once or twice a year. As leaders and coaches, we should be providing *ongoing* feedback to our people, both positive and constructive. We have an obligation to guide those in our charge, regardless of whether it feels comfortable or not. *No* employee should *ever* walk away from an annual review session blindsided by the outcome—not if they have received meaningful performance coaching throughout the year.

Beyond regular performance discussions, people also look to their leaders to help shepherd their professional growth and learning opportunities. Twice in my career, I have had the misfortune of being managed by a boss who demonstrated zero interest in supporting my career development. On the contrary, their primary concern seemed fixated on how I could make *them* look good and how I could personally contribute to *their* long-term success. Apparently, it never dawned on them that by helping foster my growth, they could have personally reaped the benefits of a more competent, capable, and valued teammate. Instead, their lack of support resulted in my pursuing opportunities elsewhere.

As leaders and coaches, we have an obligation to create a work environment where team members thrive. Research regarding the efficacy of traditional performance review methods certainly reinforces the need for substantive change. A 2016 study conducted by the Society for Human Resources Management revealed that 95 percent of employees are unhappy with their organizational appraisal process and only 10 percent believe the reviews provide accurate information.[11]

So, what is the optimal way to manage the performance review dilemma? A growing number of organizations, including Microsoft and Cigna, have done away with traditional reviews and have transitioned to frequent check-ins focused on goals, growth, and continuous feedback.

Here are some best practices to consider as you evaluate the effectiveness of your performance appraisal process:

- Devise an employee appraisal system organized around timely, structured, and ongoing performance discussions. Use these regular touch-base sessions to embrace the power of feedback. It is good for all parties involved: the company, the manager, and the team member. An impressive 43 percent of highly engaged employees receive feedback at least once a week, compared to only 18 percent of employees with low engagement.[12]

- Ongoing performance feedback is of particular importance to millennials and upcoming Gen Z employees. Millennials prefer to receive feedback a startling 50 percent more often than their non-millennial peers, and alarmingly they indicate that 46 percent of managers fall short in that request. With millennials alone expected to comprise more than three-fourths of the global workforce by 2025, we cannot afford to underestimate the importance of regular feedback.[13]

- Not only do younger people entering the workforce want (and expect) to have regular performance dialogue with their leader, they also want to know that their specific work role is making a noteworthy difference to the customers they serve and their broader community and world. Millennial and Generation Z employees have an expectation that supervisors will partner with them to grow their influence and impact. Be sure to establish healthy guardrails with your team members here, proactively supporting and helping guide their professional goals and ambitions while also clearly articulating their responsibility to take personal control of their careers.

- Over time, I have observed numerous cases where managers were offered no formal training on how to conduct effective performance review and development discussions. Though we fully expect our leaders to manage team-member growth and development, we inexplicably fail to equip them with the tools and resources required to do so.

Collaborate with your learning and HR professionals to design a training solution that teaches leaders performance management essentials, particularly those involving tough conversations where negative feedback is required. I recommend you follow a "know, show, do" strategy as part of your training design. First, make sure trainees *know* the basics for conducting regular performance coaching sessions. Next, move beyond the conceptual, and walk participants through multiple scenarios that *show* them how feedback sessions should look and sound. Ask for volunteers to join you during training sessions to role-play common feedback scenarios.

Devise SMARTER Goals

Effective goal setting allows your workforce to keep proper score and drive for continuous improvement. When establishing performance goals or objectives, I recommend following the SMARTER method. Here is an overview of the acronym:

- **Specific.** Goals should be as objective as possible by answering who, what, when, and where. Simply "knowing intuitively" or "feeling it in your gut" is not a sufficient strategy. For example, we might position a goal statement as follows: "By March 1, 2022, Jimmy will successfully implement the new Evergreen payroll software, based upon aggregated defect reporting of no more than 3.2 percent."

- **Measurable.** Neglecting to include metrics as part of your goal statements would be like playing a baseball game without tracking any relevant statistics (number of strikes, number of outs, number of runs, etc.). Without "hard" measures, it is simply impossible to gauge real performance or develop objective improvement strategies. This practice tends to be even more pervasive in support of operational units that do not lend themselves to conventional sales or financial metrics. When all is said and done, all team members should be able to answer the question "Am I winning?"

- **Achievable.** Goals should balance being too conservative versus being too aggressive. Few things are more demoralizing to team members than mandating goals that are clearly impossible to attain. I am reminded of the concept of *learned helplessness*, a term originally coined by psychologists Martin Seligman and Steven F. Maier. Seligman and Maier observed helpless behavior in dogs who over time were conditioned to anticipate an electrical shock after hearing a specific tone. Sensing that they could not affect an improved outcome, the dogs eventually stopped trying to avoid the shock altogether, even when opportunities for change become readily available.[14]

- **Relevant.** Goals established at the individual or local level should always align with higher-level organizational strategies. Failing to make this important connection is a surefire way to exasperate your workforce. When in doubt, leaders should ask themselves whether a goal in question (or pathway to achieve it) will ultimately contribute to the overall company success strategy.

- **Timely.** A seemingly suitable goal should also be reevaluated if it cannot be achieved within a reasonable time frame. It becomes increasingly difficult to maintain passion and momentum for any performance metric when the time horizon for attaining it is too distant in the future. What's more, the environment and circumstances under which the goal was initially established might completely change over a prolonged time period. If you conclude a long-range goal is still the right way to go, consider breaking it into subgoals with shorter time horizons.

- **Evaluate.** Just as performance discussions should take place on a regular basis, so, too, should an assessment of the efficacy and durability of the goals themselves. Ask yourself the following questions as part of a regular goal evaluation process: Have unanticipated technological or economic disruptions forced your organization to reconsider its path forward? Do your customer listening tools (surveys, focus groups, interviews, social media posts, etc.) suggest a subtle shift in client expectations and requirements? Have competitive threats caused senior leadership to question the strength of your current value proposition? If the answer to any of these questions is yes or even maybe, you should consider the need to readjust accordingly.

- **Readjust.** Embracing the notion that goals should be regularly evaluated for relevancy and soundness is great, but it is an obvious waste of time and effort in the absence of taking real action. Sadly, many organizations fail to coach their leaders on the importance of readjusting performance objectives when necessary, and as a result the goals become stagnant or even irrelevant.

Reinforce Core Values

In tandem with establishing a set of SMARTER goals to help drive performance discussions, it is also imperative that all team members be regularly coached regarding their ability to operationalize the organization's core values. These core values (often referred to as competencies) are strategic guideposts for evaluating right from wrong and determining acceptable from unacceptable. Core values bring an enterprise's noble purpose to life.

Unlike individual and corporate goals, which will regularly shift or recalibrate as a result of attainment or evolving environmental factors, core values should rarely if ever change, even in the face of great adversity or disruption. When properly knitted into the cultural fabric of your institution, values direct the essential decisions and behaviors of the workforce.

Ensure adherence to company values is hardwired into your organization's overall talent management framework, including a designated section within your appraisal template and as part of coaching guidelines for regular performance dialogue.

Final Thoughts

Here are some final points for consideration in your organizational quest to develop and retain a tribe of highly motivated, purpose-driven employees who cannot imagine working anywhere else:

- Consistently explore opportunities to expose top performers to other areas of the company through special projects, cross-functional committees, job shadowing, etc.
- Invest in a good organizational LMS (learning management system) that allows for the easy deployment and tracking of online educational programs.
- Budget ample dollars to reward high-performing employees with admission to industry conferences and seminars.

- Support employees in identifying and becoming board members of local for-profit or nonprofit organizations. Encourage active community volunteerism.
- Purchase an organizational subscription to an online learning/content platform such as LinkedIn Learning or Udemy.
- Provide tuition reimbursement opportunities for degree-based or continuing education courses.
- Start an organizational or departmental book club.

Next Steps on the Pathway-to-Purpose Journey

→ **Do you believe your organization is *obsessed* with continuous learning?** Would your fellow leaders agree with your assessment? How about frontline employees? What steps will you take to further develop a culture of learning? Ask your leadership team the question WD-40 CEO Garry Ridge regularly asks his people: "When is the last time you did something for the first time?"

→ **Confidentially survey a subset of employees from across the enterprise to gauge perceptions of your current organizational performance review process.** As part of the questionnaire, elicit feedback regarding the frequency and general effectiveness of performance review discussions between respondents and their managers. Aggregate the survey data to identify key themes, and partner with your senior leadership team to design an action plan and timeline for improved performance dialogue.

→ **Conduct a talent review session to collectively assess the current performance and future potential of your most critical enterprise-wide leadership roles.** Consider bringing in an external facilitator with expertise in 9-box talent methodology to guide the process, ensuring the team remains objective and on task throughout.

→ **Is leadership development a top priority in your organization?** Ask your executive team to review the development strategies outlined in this chapter. Come to a consensus on ways to improve your leader development program that can be implemented successfully within the next thirty days.

CONCLUSION

South of mainland Japan, where the East China Sea meets the Pacific Ocean, lies the magnificent island of Okinawa. Also known as the "Hawaii of Japan," Okinawa is a paradise for marine life, and it serves as a backdrop for some of the best snorkeling and scuba-diving anywhere. But there is another reason the island is famous. Life expectancies per capita are longer in Okinawa than anywhere else on the planet. The island also boasts the largest population of people living to age one-hundred or older. Native Okinawans don't just live longer; they are generally happier, healthier, and more at peace than the rest of us.

There are numerous environmental factors that could help explain this phenomenon, including healthy dietary habits, strong social connectedness and regular physical activity. Irrespective of these factors, historians and cultural anthropologists widely theorize that something even bigger is at play when it comes to their extended lifespans. It has to do with the prevalence of a deeply ingrained philosophy on the island known as *ikigai* (pronounced ick-ee-guy). Loosely translated, ikigai means "reason for living," or more broadly, the "happiness derived from being busy at some activity that holds deep meaning."

Realizing your ikigai is most often achieved at the intersection of four primary elements:

- What you love *(your passion)*
- What you are good at *(your talent)*
- What you can get paid to do *(your career)*
- What the world needs from you *(your purpose)*

There is nothing magical in considering these statements separately in isolation. But when we thoughtfully evaluate them together, as integral parts of a greater whole, the power of ikigai is truly ignited! It makes a ton of sense when you think about it. As a leader, wouldn't you want every one of your team members to love what they do, and at the same time be excellent at it? This blend of employee passion and talent is always a winning formula. It's a formula that smart organizations are more than willing to pay for to ensure retention of their top talent.

Imagine what might be possible, though, if your most valuable employees also clearly understood how their efforts aligned with a cause much bigger than themselves? As we've discussed previously, the possibilities resulting from this interpersonal and organizational shift are limitless! Pivoting from a perspective of making a living to making a difference will radically transform your culture.

In wrapping up our time together, it is my sincere hope that this book will serve as a blueprint for designing the type of workplace you have always wanted for yourself and your colleagues. Whether you are sitting squarely in the C-suite or just leading yourself, leverage the ideas outlined in this book to help craft the next great chapter in the life of your organization.

As discussed throughout, there is no fast pass mechanism or eventual finish line on the pathway to purpose. The journey is long and arduous, but it is always worth it. When the relentless pressures of the daily grind threaten to hijack your bigger story, it's perfectly natural to become distracted, disappointed, and even disillusioned. But stay the course. Burn the boats. And remain true to your noble purpose. Make sure the story you are writing today will be worth telling tomorrow. Craft a story that you, your team, and your customers will find... irresistible.

> There is no passion to be found in living small—in
> settling for a life that is anything less than
> what you are capable of living.
> —Nelson Mandela

NOTES

Introduction

1. Stephen M. R. Covey, *The Speed of Trust* (New York: Free Press, 2006), 225.
2. Joy L. Woodson, "All Hail the Popsicle," *Patch Media,* April 26, 2012, https://patch.com/georgia/snellville/all-hail-the-popsicle-king-of-pops.
3. Doug Claffey, interview by author, January 2020.
4. John Kotter and James Heskett, *Corporate Culture and Performance* (New York: Free Press, 1992), 78.

Chapter 1

1. Jim Harter, "4 Factors Driving Record-High Employee Engagement in U.S." *Gallup.com,* November 5, 2020, https://www.gallup.com/workplace/284180/factors-driving-record-high-employee-engagement.aspx.
2. Lisa McLeod, "The Rep Who Sells with Noble Purpose (and Why Competitors Should Be Afraid)," *McLeod & More,* February 10, 2016, https://www.mcleodandmore.com/2011/10/31/the-sales-rep-who-loved-and-why-you-should-be-very-afraid/.
3. Viktor E. Frankl, In Man's Search for Meaning: An Introduction to Logotherapy (Boston: Beacon Press, 2006), 97–109.

Chapter 2

1. Peter Gasca, "For Entrepreneurial Success, Burn Your Boats," *Inc.com,* April 30, 2018, https://www.inc.com/peter-gasca/for-entrepreneurial-success-burn-your-boats.html.
2. Bruce Jones, "The Difference between Purpose and Mission," *Jbilly.com,* 2016, https://jbilly.com/the-difference-between-purpose-and-mission-sponsor-content-from-disney-institute/.
3. Sally Blount, "Why Are We Here?" *HBR.com,* November 17, 2019, https://hbr.org/2019/11/why-are-we-here.
4. Ibid.
5. Kate Taylor, "The Church of Chicken: The Inside Story of How Chick-fil-A Used Christian Values and a 'Clone Army' to Build a Booming Business That's Defying the Retail Apocalypse and Taking over America," *Business Insider,* August 8, 2019, https://www.businessinsider.com/how-chick-fil-a-took-over-america-2019-8.
6. Perry McGuire, *Nice, but Not Naïve* (Georgia: Brentwood Publisher's Group, 2018), 126.
7. Trisha Henry, "Human Factor: Horst Schulze," *CNN,* December 28, 2010, https://thechart.blogs.cnn.com/2010/12/28/human-factor-horst-schulze/.
8. Aimee Lucas, "Want Employees Who Are All-In?," *American Banker,* August 28, 2018, https://www.americanbanker.com/opinion/want-employees-who-are-all-in.

Chapter 3

1. Matthew 7:24–27 (New International Version).
2. James L. Heskett et al., The Service Profit Chain: How Leading Companies Link Profit and Growth to Loyalty, Satisfaction, and Value (New York: The Free Press, 1997).
3. Patrick Lencioni, "The Untapped Advantage of Organizational Health," webinar from EntreLeadership, May 28, 2020.

4. Carol Dweck, "The Power of Believing That You Can Improve," TED, November 2014, https://www.ted.com/talks/carol_dweck_the_power_of_believing_that_you_can_improve.
5. David Naylor, the Motivational Intelligence Southeast Conference, September 20, 2019.
6. David Burkus, "A Tale of Two Cultures: Why Culture Trumps Core Values in Building Ethical Organizations," *Journal of JBVL*, Winter/Spring 2011, http://www.valuesbasedleadershipjournal.com/issues/vol4issue1/tale_2culture.php.
7. Sophie Hart, "Vulnerability-Based Trust: The First Behavior of a Cohesive Team," *Serenity Collective,* April 25, 2018, https://theserenitycollective.com/vulnerability-based-trust/.
8. Executive Summary, "Employee Job Satisfaction and Engagement: The Doors of Opportunity Are Open," *SHRM*, 2017, https://www.shrm.org/hr-today/trends-and-forecasting/research-and-surveys/Documents/2017-Employee-Job-Satisfaction-and-Engagement-Executive-Summary.pdf.
9. Barry D. Schwartz, "Rethinking Work," *New York Times*, August 28, 2015, https://www.nytimes.com/2015/08/30/opinion/sunday/rethinking-work.html.
10. Bruce N. Pfau, "How an Accounting Firm Convinced Its Employees They Could Change the World," *Harvard Business Review*, November–December 2017, https://hbr.org/2015/10/how-an-accounting-firm-convinced-its-employees-they-could-change-the-world.
11. Thomas J. Peters and Robert H. Waterman, *In Search of Excellence* (London: Profile Books, 2015), 289.

Chapter 4
1. Shawn Achor, *Big Potential: How Transforming the Pursuit of Success Raises Our Achievement, Happiness, and Well-Being* (New York: Crown, 2018), 23.

2. Shawn Achor et al., "Collaborative Overload," *Harvard Business Review*, January–February 2016, https://hbr.org/2016/01/collaborative-overload.

3. Kathleen McAuliffe, "The Undiscovered World of Thomas Edison," *Atlantic Media Company*, February 8, 2019, https://www.theatlantic.com/magazine/archive/1995/12/the-undiscovered-world-of-thomas-edison/305880/.

4. Charles Duhigg, "What Google Learned from Its Quest to Build the Perfect Team," *New York Times*, February 28, 2016, https://www.nytimes.com/2016/02/28/magazine/what-google-learned-from-its-quest-to-build-the-perfect-team.html.

5. Ibid.

6. Ibid.

7. Ibid.

8. Henry Blodget, "In a Revealing Interview with Henry Blodget, Ray Dalio Offers a Radical Solution to the Threat of 'Fake News' and Details Life inside Bridgewater," *Business Insider*, January 7, 2017, https://www.businessinsider.com/ray-dalio-interview-henry-blodget-1-2017.

9. Ray Dalio, *Principles* (New York: Simon & Schuster, 2017), 339.

10. Glenn Llopis, "The New England Patriots: The Mastery of Teamwork in a Climate of Constant Change," *Forbes Magazine*, February 7, 2019, https://www.forbes.com/sites/glennllopis/2019/02/06/the-new-england-patriots-the-mastery-of-teamwork-in-a-climate-of-constant-change/.

11. Ayse Birsel, "WD-40 Does $380 Million in Sales a Year. Its Secret Sauce Is Surprisingly Simple," *Inc.com*, March 30, 2018, https://www.inc.com/ayse-birsel/how-wd-40-does-380-million-in-sales-a-year-by-living-these-3-key-values.html.

12. James Peltz, "Q&A: WD-40 CEO Garry Ridge Explains Company's Slick Success," *Los Angeles Times*, July 30, 2015, https://www.latimes.com/business/la-fi-qa-wd-40-20150730-story.html.

13. Brene Brown, "The Power of Vulnerability," TED, June 2010, https://www.ted.com/talks/brene_brown_the_power_of_vulnerability?language=en.

14. John Saddington, "On Knowing the Real Story," *John Saddington*, April 17, 2015, https://john.do/real-story/.

15. Kaitlyn S. C Hatch et al., "Why Do Toddlers Bother Learning to Walk?" *Research Digest*, July 30, 2016, https://digest.bps.org.uk/2012/12/18/why-do-toddlers-bother-learning-to-walk/.

16. Simon Sinek, *Leaders Eat Last* (London: Penguin Business, 2017), 97.

Chapter 5

1. Geoffrey James, "Top 40 Bonehead Boss Stories," *CBS Interactive*, October 28, 2011, https://www.cbsnews.com/news/top-40-bonehead-boss-stories/.

2. Dan Pontefract et al., "9 Out of 10 People Are Willing to Earn Less Money to Do More-Meaningful Work," *Harvard Business Review*, November 6, 2018, https://hbr.org/2018/11/9-out-of-10-people-are-willing-to-earn-less-money-to-do-more-meaningful-work.

3. Gene Marks, "Monster Poll: 76 Percent of Job Seekers Say Their Boss Is 'Toxic,'" *Inc.com*, October 18, 2018, https://www.inc.com/gene-marks/monster-poll-76-percent-of-job-seekers-say-their-boss-is-toxic.html.

4. Brandon Gaille, "9 Shocking Statistics about Bad Bosses," *BrandonGaille.com*, June 1, 2017, https://brandongaille.com/8-shocking-statistics-about-bad-bosses/.

5. Ibid.

6. Geoffrey James, "Top 40 Bonehead Boss Stories," *CBS Interactive*, October 28, 2011, https://www.cbsnews.com/news/top-40-bonehead-boss-stories/.

7. Jim Clifton and James K. Harter, It's the Manager: Gallup Finds the Quality of Managers and Team Leaders Is the Single Biggest

Factor in Your Organization's Long-Term Success (New York: Gallup Press, 2019), 107.

8. Atul Gawande, "The Coach in the Operating Room," *New Yorker*, September 26, 2011, https://www.newyorker.com/magazine/2011/10/03/personal-best.

9. Geoffrey James, "Top 40 Bonehead Boss Stories," *CBS Interactive*, October 28, 2011, https://www.cbsnews.com/news/top-40-bonehead-boss-stories/.

10. Anupum Pant, "The Role of Wind in a Tree's Life," *Awesci*, December 29, 2014, http://awesci.com/the-role-of-wind-in-a-trees-life/.

11. John Montopoli, "Public Speaking Anxiety and Fear of Brain Freezes," *National Social Anxiety Center*, February 20, 2017, https://nationalsocialanxietycenter.com/2017/02/20/public-speaking-and-fear-of-brain-freezes/.

12. Michael K. Simpson, Unlocking Potential: 7 Coaching Skills That Transform Individuals, Teams, and Organizations (Michigan: Grand Harbor Press, 2014), 114.

13. Michelle Konstantinovsky, "The Mighty Banyan Tree Can 'Walk' and Live for Centuries," *HowStuffWorks*, April 2, 2020, https://science.howstuffworks.com/life/botany/understanding-roots-banyan-tree.htm.

14. Jim Clifton and James K. Harter, It's the Manager: Gallup Finds the Quality of Managers and Team Leaders Is the Single Biggest Factor in Your Organization's Long-Term Success (New York: Gallup Press, 2019), 81.

15. Veronica Craig, "8 Can't-Miss Gallup Employee Engagement Stats to Help Your Call Center," *Sharpen*, November 30, 2020, https://sharpencx.com/blog/gallup-employee-engagement-key-statistics/.

Chapter 6

1. Stephen Newland, "The Power of Accountability," November 27, 2018, https://www.afcpe.org/news-and-publications/the-standard/2018-3/the-power-of-accountability/.

2. Simon Sinek, *Leaders Eat Last* (London: Penguin Business, 2017), 23–30.

3. Anne Loehr, "Why Accountability Is a Must for Teamwork and How to Create It," *AnneLoehr.com*, June 8, 2017, https://www.anneloehr.com/2017/06/08/accountability-a-must-for-teamwork/.

Chapter 7

1. Lori McKnight, "Council Post: Recognition Is Essential, Now More than Ever," *Forbes Magazine*, March 26, 2020, https://www.forbes.com/sites/forbescommunicationscouncil/2020/03/26/recognition-is-essential-now-more-than-ever/?sh=360d1c745c0e.

2. "More than Half of Employees Would Stay Longer at Their Company if Bosses Showed More Appreciation," November 3, 2013, Glassdoor, https://www.glassdoor.com/about-us/employees-stay-longer-company-bosses-showed-appreciation-glassdoor-survey/.

3. Ibid.

4. Danielle Cronquist, "3 Important Differences between Reward and Recognition," *BambooHR,* December 18, 2019, https://www.bamboohr.com/blog/difference-reward-and-recognition/.

5. Sharon Florentine, "What Really Motivates Workers? (It's Not Always Money)," *CIO*, April 27, 2016, https://www.cio.com/article/3062056/what-really-motivates-workers-its-not-always-money.html.

6. Frederick Herzberg, "One More Time: How Do You Motivate Employees?" *Harvard Business Review*, January 2003, https://hbr.org/2003/01/one-more-time-how-do-you-motivate-employees.

7. Daniel H. Pink, *Drive: The Surprising Truth about What Motivates Us* (Scotland: Canongate Books, 2018), 13–19.
8. Ibid., 28.
9. Ibid., 75.
10. HR Daily Advisor Content Team, "Workers Willing to Compromise on Salary for the Right Benefits, Culture, and Growth Opportunities," *HR Daily Advisor*, April 13, 2018, https://hrdailyadvisor.blr.com/2017/10/20/workers-willing-compromise-salary-right-benefits-culture-growth-opportunities/.
11. Peter Economy, "The (Millennial) Workplace of the Future Is Almost Here—These 3 Things Are About to Change Big Time," *Inc.com*, January 15, 2019, https://www.inc.com/peter-economy/the-millennial-workplace-of-future-is-almost-here-these-3-things-are-about-to-change-big-time.html.
12. Udemy Report, "Udemy In Depth: 2018 Millennials at Work Report," *Udemy Research*, April 2019, research.udemy.com/research_report/udemy-in-depth-2018-millennials-at-work-report/.
13. Malcolm Gladwell, *Outliers* (London: Penguin, 2009), 116–58.
14. Chip Bell and John Patterson, "Customer Value," *ChipBell.com*, June 2, 2015, https://www.taketheirbreathaway.com/customer-value/what-can-lexus-teach-us-about-service-2/.

Chapter 8

1. Elliot Kennel, "Why Cleveland Browns Former Tackle Joe Thomas Is Truly One of Us," *FanSided*, May 15, 2020, https://dawgpounddaily.com/2020/05/15/why-cleveland-browns-joe-thomas-is-truly-one-of-us/.
2. Matthew Florjancic, "Former Cleveland Browns Count Themselves Fortunate to Call Joe Thomas a Teammate," *Wkyc.com*, March 19, 2018, https://www.wkyc.com/article/sports/nfl/browns/former-cleveland-browns-count-themselves-fortunate-to-call-joe-thomas-a-teammate/95-529903181.

3. Peter King, "Joe Thomas' NFL Snaps Streak: Five Things to Know," *SI.com*, September 18, 2017, https://www.si.com/ nfl/2017/09/18/joe-thomas-cleveland-browns-nfl-snaps-plays-streak.

4. Jude Scinta, "Personality Assessments Foster Individual and Team Success," *Advisors Magazine*, August 10, 2018, http:// www.advisorsmagazine.com/business/245-ceo-insights/22983-personality-assessments-foster-individual-and-team-success.

5. Roberta Matuson, Evergreen Talent a Guide to Hiring and Cultivating a Sustainable Workforce (Massachusetts: Career Press, 2020), 26.

6. Erin Blog, "Employee Referral Statistics You Need to Know for 2020 (Infographic)," *ERIN*, January 7, 2020, https://erinapp. com/wp-content/uploads/2019/02/erinlogo_620.png, January 7, 2020. https://erinapp.com/recruitment/employee-referral-statistics-you-need-to-know-for-2020/.

7. Kristina Martic, "4 Companies with the Best Employee Referral Awards," *Medium.com*, August 3, 2018, https://medium.com/ hr-blog-resources/4-companies-with-the-best-employee-referral-awards-57d711ff0c6c.

8. Ryan O'Donnell, "Template: How to Hire Like Google (Hint: Their Secret Is Employee Referrals)," *EmployUs*, December 31, 2019, https://employus.com/blog/google.

9. Jude Scinta, "Personality Assessments Foster Individual and Team Success," *Advisors Magazine*, August 10, 2018, http:// www.advisorsmagazine.com/business/245-ceo-insights/22983-personality-assessments-foster-individual-and-team-success.

10. Gina Belli, "These Companies Pay Unhappy Workers to Quit," *PayScale*, September 19, 2018, https://www.payscale.com/career-news/2018/09/these-companies-pay-unhappy-workers-to-quit.

11. Oxford Briefing, "What a Shoe Shop Can Teach Us about Developing High Performance Cultures," *Oxford Review*, March 7, 2017, https://www.oxford-review.com/shoe-shop-can-teach-us-developing-high-performance-cultures/.

Chapter 9

1. Chip Heath and Dan Heath, The Power of Moments: Why
   Certain Experiences Have Extraordinary Impact (New York:
   Simon & Schuster, 2019), 20–22.

2. Arlene S. Hirsch, "Don't Underestimate the Importance of
   Good Onboarding," *SHRM*, July 30, 2020, https://www.shrm.
   org/resourcesandtools/hr-topics/talent-acquisition/pages/dont-
   underestimate-the-importance-of-effective-onboarding.aspx.

3. Steve Tobak, "8 Great Entrepreneurial Success Stories,"
   Entrepreneur, February 28, 2015, https://www.entrepreneur.com/
   article/243099.

4. Patrick Moorhead, "Cisco's 'People Deal' Exemplifies
   Its Cutting Edge Commitment to Employees," *Forbes
   Magazine*, August 8, 2018, https://www.forbes.com/sites/
   patrickmoorhead/2018/08/08/ciscos-people-deal-exemplifies-its-
   cutting-edge-commitment-to-employees/.

5. Team Panopto, "How Long Should Your Employee Onboarding
   Process Be?," *Panopto Video Platform*, August 23, 2020, https://
   www.panopto.com/blog/how-long-should-your-employee-
   onboarding-program-be/.

6. Bill Taylor, "How WD-40 Created a Learning-Obsessed
   Company Culture," *Harvard Business Review*, September 16,
   2016, https://hbr.org/2016/09/how-wd-40-created-a-learning-
   obsessed-company-culture.

7. Marshall Goldsmith, *What Got You Here Won't Get You There*
   (New York: Hyperion, 2007), 42–43.

8. Nicola Cronin, "Mentoring Statistics: The Research You Need
   to Know," *Online Mentoring Software*, February 2, 2020, https://
   www.guider-ai.com/blog/mentoring-statistics-the-research-you-
   need-to-know/.

9. Ibid.

10. Ibid.

11. Dori Meinert, "Is It Time to Put the Performance Review on a
    PIP?" *SHRM*, April 1, 2015, https://www.shrm.org/hr-today/

news/hr-magazine/pages/0415-qualitative-performance-reviews.
aspx.

12. Rich Lyons, "Feedback: You Need to Lead It," *Forbes*, July 10,
2017, https://www.forbes.com/sites/richlyons/2017/07/10/
feedback-you-need-to-lead-it/?sh=7da5c8c74a35.

13. Karie Willyerd, "Millennials Want to Be Coached at Work,"
Harvard Business Review, December 6, 2017, https://hbr.
org/2015/02/millennials-want-to-be-coached-at-work.

14. Kendra Cherry, "What Causes Learned Helplessness?" *Verywell
Mind*, June 7, 2020, https://www.verywellmind.com/what-is-
learned-helplessness-2795326.

ACKNOWLEDGEMENTS

Writing *Pathway to Purpose* has been both an exhausting and an exhilarating effort. It is the realization of a long-held passion to equip others with a roadmap for designing workplaces of distinction. Over the years, I've been blessed to work with (and learn from) some extraordinary business leaders and their respective organizations. These collective experiences have largely shaped my perspectives around organizational culture.

Even with the broad insights gleaned from my past, this book would not have been possible without the enduring support of an amazing tribe of loved ones and colleagues. I first want to recognize my amazing wife Julie for being such a powerful source of encouragement. Thanks for always lifting me up when I had major doubts regarding this project. Special kudos as well to my precious daughters Madalyn, Elaina, and Juliana. I appreciate you lending me your masterful editing skills and content ideas! I would also be remiss if I didn't express my gratitude to Mom and Dad for always believing in me, even during those times when I struggled to believe in myself.

Next, I want to acknowledge the core team from Palmetto Publishing who helped guide me through all the nuances of the book publishing process. Of particular note are Stephanie Stupalski, Abbey Suchoski and Travis Crane. Thanks to each of you for fielding my incessant questions and requests!

Numerous friends and business associates deserve recognition for their wise counsel, raw candor and collective voice of reason along the way. These individuals include Annette Rollins, Roberta Matuson, Lisa McLeod,

Marshal Goldsmith, Richard Tiller, Ike Reighard, Doug Williams, Lior Arussy, Roy Heintz, Pat Williams, Jim Kouzes and Chester Elton.

There are two people who deserve special recognition. These individuals read my manuscript from cover to cover, providing detailed feedback and expert counsel on how to most effectively bring this book to life. To Renee Maxwell and Chip Bell, thanks from the bottom of my heart!

Last but certainly not least, I want to publicly thank Jesus Christ for planting the seeds of purpose in my heart. For this, I am eternally grateful.

ABOUT THE AUTHOR

Jamey Lutz is a noted author, speaker and facilitator with expertise in the disciplines of organizational culture change, customer loyalty and employee engagement. He currently serves as Managing Director of Service Excellence with ChenMed, a healthcare company committed to transforming care of senior citizens in the neediest populations.

Lutz previously worked in numerous leadership and performance excellence roles for the Orlando Magic, Ritz-Carlton Hotel Company, HomeBanc Mortgage, Forrest Performance Group and Atlantic Capital. He and his family live in Alpharetta, Georgia.

To learn more about Jamey Lutz and available resources, please visit jameylutz.com.

CPSIA information can be obtained
at www.ICGtesting.com
Printed in the USA
FSHW021123220421
80591FS